management in quandary

a critique of organizational power

ROSS JACKSON

Library of Congress Control Number: 2022901163

FIRST EDITION

ISBN: 979-8-9856243-0-4

Published in Tipp City, Ohio
Printed in the United States of America

DEDICATION

To all those engaged in the prolonged struggle for greater authenticity and autonomy at work

management in quandary

a critique of organizational power

Contents

Prologue: Management Deconstructed · · · · · · · · · · · · · · · · · · · ix

I. Squares in Cubes · 1

II. The Unbearable Banality of Management · · · · · · · · · · · · · · 23

III. The Spectacle of Work · 45

IV. Devolving Slowly · 67

V. A Path Forward · 91

Epilogue: Towards Authenticity & Autonomy · · · · · · · · · · · · · 123

References · 129

Author Biography · 145

Prologue: Management Deconstructed

Power resides at the core of management theory and praxis. Entangled in dynamic interrelationships of management, one is ultimately organizationally reduced to being a superior or a subordinate and frequently confronts the tensions as well as the contradictions associated with inhabiting both of those roles simultaneously. Through such an interplay, power is exerted to coerce or *incentivize* individuals. This is stated transparently in the definition of management as the discipline focused on accomplishing tasks and achieving goals using the planning, organizing, staffing, directing, and controlling functions, processes, and resources. Unpacking such an amalgam requires effort. Narrowing the focus on this definition, one can see clearly and directly that an asserted function of management is to *control* (*human*) resources. This assertion to the right of control warrants scrutiny. What other modern discipline rests on a claimed foundation that it is justifiable and desirable to control other humans? In academic fields such as political science, sociology, and philosophy such an assertion would be seized upon immediately for theoretical critique and rigorous debate. For those educated, engaged, or otherwise interested in business, the legitimacy of management's claim of control likely seems as self-evident as it is unproblematic. The critique of organizational power presented here aims to change the passive acceptance of that assertion. Placing management in quandary in this regard is important for those studying business and management, and for those who are dissatisfied in their career. These are the individuals who are most likely to benefit from joining the prolonged struggle for greater authenticity and autonomy at work. What follows is an exploration of this concern. Deconstruction is the lens through which this critique of the phenomenon of management as an ideology is enacted.

Deconstruction is elusive. The meanings and aims of *deconstruction*, as a methodological approach, are varied and at times contradictory. As a result, it is useful to state explicitly how deconstruction is applied here to analyze management. Most directly, deconstruction is a method of critical analysis focused on interrelationships between *texts* and *meanings*. Specifically, this work is focused on a critique of organizational power which resides in and around the theory and praxis of management as an ideology. In the dyadic relationship between superior and subordinate, it is relatively clear how a worker is routinely subjugated by management. Literally, subordinates are customarily told what to do. But what of the manager? As a starting point, and as already noted, since managers are most frequently also subordinates, the same subjugation is always potentially in play, simply at a higher echelon within an organization. Additionally, being engaged in the role and function of management is potentially a source of alienation as a manager gives embodiment and voice to organizational views which may be inconsistent with one's own. Placing management in quandary reveals *subjugation* and *alienation* for both managers and the managed. These two dynamics constrain performance and reduce individual well-being and are important considerations existentially and organizationally. And yet for all this subjugation and alienation, there is no shortage of those willing to engage in this form of employment. In fact, one might consider this a normal part of *doing* business. This suggests management is an ideology rather than simply a discipline, function, or position. In confronting this, what is one who wants to be in business to do?

If such a dynamic is inherent in management itself, if one is going to be engaged in business, it might be difficult or impossible to avoid the dual consequences of subjugation and alienation. However, such a conclusion is too bleak to consider. Work can, of course, be sites of drudgery and official relationships ones of overt and covert coercion, but this doesn't need to be the case. While the functions of management are essential, embodying those functions in an individual is not. One can make work a place in which self-expression and creativity flourish and collegiality is the norm. Doing so requires a thorough understanding of *management-as-a-given*, that is as an *ideology*, as well as a vision as to how one might reasonably reform this situation and work towards the creation of a viable alternative. This work is aimed towards the establishment of such an understanding and the radical redefinition of what it means to be engaged in and with management. To address this concern, management is addressed in some of its various manifestations from both the perspective of the manager and the managed. At each turn, the focus is directed towards a critique of organizational power and management as an ideology. Only by understanding asymmetries of power and its persistence in management, can one hope to avoid its most inhumane consequences and reimagine something ennobling in its place. To accomplish this goal the context for this critique of organizational power requires further delimitation.

This critique is focused primarily on management as it is enacted within the United States of America in professional or general office settings. Situating the context of this critique of organizational power thusly was determined for a variety of reasons. The situation faced by workers in the United States is complex. Whereas there are opportunities to advance, and success (as typically defined as career advancement) is rewarded with wealth, prestige, and power, many people who work hard experience seemingly unnecessary adversities and deprivations. These hardships are reported routinely by the media. A few statistics related to employment in the United States provide contours as to the situation faced by its workers. In terms of real wages (i.e., wages adjusted for inflation), a 2020 report by the Congressional Research Service found that from the year 1979 to 2019, the wages of the top earners increased by 41.3%, whereas the wages of those in middle increased by 8.8%, and those at the bottom experienced a 6.5% wage increase. Some argue that since each group's wages increased, that each group is better off than they were previously. There is certainly some validity to that position. However, well-being has both an absolute and a relative component. The data clearly suggest that the gap between the richest and the poorest within the United States has widened from 1979 to now. Examining worker rights provides further context. Within the highly industrialized countries, the United States has among the lowest levels of rights, protections, and earned benefits for its workers. A 2019 report from the Center for Economic and Policy Research found that, "the United States continues to be the only advanced economy that does not guarantee its workers paid vacation," and that "without a federal paid vacation policy, close to one in four

Americans have no paid vacation (23 percent) and no paid holidays (22 percent)." Similarly, as of 2020, Business Insider reported that "besides Papua New Guinea, the US is the only country in the world that has no national policy guaranteeing leave for new mothers," and that "of the world's richest 41 countries, the US is one of 15 that does not offer any paternity leave." Admittedly, some organizations provide ample employee benefits, but in the absence of national requirements in the aggregate the average level of employee benefits net to a level which could be a source of collective embarrassment and action for those in the United States. The last reason, which is related to the issues of wages and benefits insofar as the situation is perpetuated without effective collective action, is that workers in the United States tend to accept unquestioningly management as an ideology. For these reasons, this critique of organizational power is most relevant to those least aware of the coerciveness of management as an ideology and who are in most need of the rewards achieved through collective engagement. Of course, these concerns are universal enough that they could be of interest to anybody engaged in professional work dynamics which are enacted using management.

With the hope of providing an understanding for informed action, this critique is divided into five sections. Section one, *squares in cubes*, is focused on management from a subordinate's perspective, whereas section two, *the unbearable banality of management*, is focused on management as experienced from a manager's perspective. Together, these two sections highlight the subjugation, alienation, and power dynamics inherent in management between superiors and subordinates. Section three, *the spectacle of work*, brings attention to the performative aspects of employment, and section four, *devolving slowly*, highlights the entropic nature of sustaining that spectacle over the duration of one's career. These two sections combine to reveal the transformations individuals experience at work, which emerge through the management structure and the corrosive effect such a construction has on the inherent dignity of all employment. Lastly, section five, *a path forward*, provides a concise exploration of how managers and the managed could enact a different way of being. Each section contains an original piece of détournement art to capture its mood and offer a point of reflection. Collectively, these five sections place management in quandary as a basis for critiquing organizational power. For those who take the inherent dignity of work and individual agency seriously, such a critique of management as an ideology is long overdue. Read, think, act; a better way awaits!

I. Squares in Cubes

Sitting all alone
Endless empty chatterbox
Four sides with no door

Ideology haunts management. In childhood when one is scared, there is a tendency to hide, to close one's eyes, to pull the covers up over one's head, to wish fearfully for the situation to pass quickly and without consequence. The haunting of management by ideology causes those engaged with and around it to respond in a similar fashion; one evades, pretends, and hopes. Management as theory and praxis, while extensively examined, is only understood partially. College textbooks present management largely from a perspective which supports and sustains the *status quo* and provides students of management only part of its story. For those engaged in its practice, management is largely accepted as offered. Collectively, these relationship towards management are facilitated by attempts to present management as a neutral discipline and to normalize both its applications and consequences. At one extreme, management is even offered as an objective science. Whereas there are certainly elements of management which one might consider to be amenable to analysis, at its core, management is about the sanctioned use of *power* in professional contexts. Its enactment, however benign, leaves traces of dressage on workers and managers alike. Few in organizations can escape its gaze. Consequently, it is beneficial for those engaged with management to understand it more completely. Prior to engaging in this critique of the organizational power enacted through management as an ideology, it is useful to provide some context related to modern organizational management.

Management is a popular topic which is extensively researched but understood incompletely. Studies related to management have focused upon a variety of topics including leadership (Irving, 2004; Martinussen & Davidsen, 2021; Pretorius, Steyn & Bond-Barnard, 2018; Ramírez, Alarcón & Knights, 2004), strategy (Al Shamsi, 2020; Angelova, 2019; Sofitra, Katsuhiko Takahashi, & Katsumi Morikawa, 2015; Quinn, 2007), teamwork (Fisher, 2007; Lewis, 1999; Wesner, Smith, & Austin, 2018) and organizational performance (Elgharbawy & Abdel-Kader, 2021; Hana & Lucie, 2015; Khaltar & Moon, 2020). These studies, and studies like them, are useful for understanding management theory and praxis. In both its academic and practitioner sense, the field of management as traditionally understood and applied is useful for those engaged in business. The longevity and ubiquity of management theory and praxis suggest something of its utility. Organizational management as conventionally defined has value, but it is not above critique. Critical management studies (CMS) takes aim at the common construction of management, revealing nuance, complexities, and contradictions (Fournier & Smith, 2012; Hudon & Rouillard, 2015; Maravelias, 2011; Parker, 2015).

There is no single definition of CMS in terms of its focus or approach, but research conducted within its paradigm often uses reflective assessments to analyze and critique underlying components of socially constructed realities. CMS is also critical of the ideological justifications of management. This critique is therefore philosophically aligned with components of CMS. With this foundation established one can examine management as an ideology. To do so critically, one benefits from understanding ideology.

Taking ideology from a broad perspective provides one with a vantage point from which to understand its characteristics more generally. For those unfamiliar with ideology in praxis, the desire to gravitate towards a linguistic linkage between the terms *ideology* and *ideas* is understandable. Such a construction, while intuitive, omits the role of organizations in the creation and maintenance of ideology. Althusser (2014) explained, "ideology does not exist in the 'world of ideas'...ideology exists in institutions and the practices specific to them...ideology exists *in apparatuses*," and, "these apparatuses...take as their objects and objectives the *individuals* who occupy the posts of the social-technical division of labor in production...Ideology therefore exists, by way of ideological apparatuses and their practices, precisely *in the practices of these individuals*" (p. 156, emphasis in original). This view of ideology suggests that individuals whose practices produce ideology through institutional apparatuses might be doing so through some sort of false consciousness. Sloterdijk (1987) described the three forms of "false consciousness" as lies, errors, and ideologies, with ideology being a form of "systematic error" (p. 15). This point reveals an extreme consequence. As suggested by Sloterdijk, ideology is not only an error, but also an institutionally perpetuated error. It is possible that ideology extends beyond false consciousness or error. For Žižek (2009), "ideology is not simply a 'false consciousness', an illusory representation of reality, it is rather this reality itself which is already conceived as 'ideological'...the very reproduction of which implies that the individuals 'do not know what they are doing'" (pp. 15-16). In examining ideology in its broadest construction, it is beneficial to focus some attention on the mechanisms used for its reproduction in societies, institutions, and organizations.

Althusser (2014) contended that ideology is maintained and reproduced within a society using both repressive state apparatuses (e.g., police, military, legal system, government) and ideological state apparatuses (e.g., colleges, churches, media, social clubs). Under Althusser's construction, repressive state apparatuses can use violent suppression against those who are considered *deviants*, whereas ideological state apparatuses produce conformity through psychosocial dynamics related to individual fears of being ostracized. Given the directness and transparency associated with the functioning of repressive state apparatuses, that topic will not be examined further; however, because they operate indirectly and the individual participates in the functioning of ideological state apparatuses, a little more consideration is warranted. This is even more concerning as ideological state apparatuses are largely the means through which ideology is enacted within professional contexts. Althusser explained, "the system made up of these organizations forms an apparatus that realizes an ideology of 'defense of the interests of...' a profession!...'Defense of the profession' is, for associations of middle employers and big employers a fig leave hiding their class objective" (p. 116). Žižek (2009), critiqued the gap between the functioning of ideological state apparatuses and the individual internalization of ideology resident in Althusser's construction through an examination of the trauma induced by repressive state apparatuses. As Žižek explained, the "external 'machine' of State Apparatuses exercises its force only in so far as it is experienced, in the unconscious economy of the subject, as a traumatic, senseless injunction," and that it this "non-integrated surplus of senseless traumatism which confers on the Law its unconditional authority" (p. 43). Management can be viewed both as an ideological state apparatus (Althusser; Žižek) and as an ideology, which is largely enacted by individuals who do so consciously in terms of structure and function, but unwittingly in terms of ideology. The mechanized institutionalization which is part and parcel of ideology makes it a useful concept for a critique of organizational power.

Narrowing the focus of ideology to management provides a useful point of inquiry for critiquing its theory and praxis. Examining management as an ideology reveals both its organizational pervasiveness and the acceptance of its legitimations. Deem and Brehony (2005) described how the "general ideologies of new managerialism are widespread in terms of their imposition and effects...serve the interests of those in management roles as well as agencies" and is "the legitimation of management for its own sake" (p. 220). The work of Deem and Brehony is useful here in at least two ways. First, they identified the *widespread* nature of management as an ideology. Second, their work highlighted that management, as an ideology, is a form of *legitimation* which benefits the organizations in which the theory and praxis of management is enacted. These two insights are of consequence for those engaged in the pursuit of greater authenticity and autonomy at work and hold implications for understanding dynamics and consequences around the execution of organizational power. These concerns are even more pressing when one considers management as an ideology as containing the types of systematic error or false consciousness resident in ideology in general (Althusser, 2014;

Sloterdijk, 1987; Žižek, 2009), since those directly involved in the enactment and maintenance of management as an ideology may do so unknowingly. Whereas this concern is of consequence at the corporate (i.e., upper echelon) and lower-echelon, managerial levels, it is of most direct concern at the individual worker level. It is at this level that the consequences of management ultimately rest and from which the management ranks are most likely filled.

Management as an ideology is consequential as it relates to individual workers and as it relates to their likely views towards career advancement. The concern as it relates to individual workers is examined further. The implications as to how management as an ideology can influence views towards career advancement are discussed in section two (*the unbearable banality of management*). Central to either manifestation is the concept of choice, as those engaged with management make decisions which shape and constrain their future. Choices, when made deliberately, reflect some form of value structure. To pick one thing over another betrays one's relative valuations of the things being compared. This is not any less true existentially as it is commercially. According to existentialist philosophy, one defines oneself through the decisions one makes, and those decisions reflect what one ultimately values. As Sartre (2007) described, "choosing to be this or that is to affirm at the same time the value of what we choose" (p. 24). This construction can be applied directly to those seeking employment. Assuming one can select from a sufficiently large number of job offers, one's choice of employment and subsequent formation of identity likely conforms to the existential ideal described by Sartre. However, in practice, one often does not have the opportunity to select from among many offers. Even if one were to receive a multitude of job offers, they tend to be disjointed in terms of their arrival and be valid for a limited time. These two things combine to make the notion that one can select the best job from a pool of competing offers largely untenable. For recent graduates or those who are currently unemployed, one is looking simply for a job, *any job*, that falls within a given spectrum of one's available skill set and desired pay range. In short, one might pragmatically decide to settle for a job which is considered by the individual to be just good enough for the time being. In the strictest sense, existentialist philosophers would correctly assert that given such a *satisficing* decision, one has still made a choice and is therefore committed without excuse. The harshness of that existential position is potentially beneficial in terms of strengthening one's resolve and agency; however, it does little to bolster the compassion and empathy we could hold for each other. Navigating career and life is challenging. To a degree, no matter the outcome or how it might appear to an outside observer, people are generally doing the best they can. People make decisions with incomplete information and hope for the best. What more can one do? Such fumbling, while observable throughout, is perhaps clearest at the beginning of one's career trajectory.

Starting one's career can be a unique and special time filled with both uncertainty and excitement. Often there is a feeling of gratitude for the opportunity to work and happiness associated with having some degree of security. Landing one's first *real job* (i.e., the position which starts one's career rather than a string of temporary and largely lateral, entry-level jobs) is viewed as an important step in one's personal and professional development. The position potentially provides one with a new sense of *self*. At a minimum, the job provides a new aspect to incorporate into one's identity. Initially, one is curious about the work, the people within the organization, and is hopeful for opportunities to make meaningful contributions that support future career advancement. The length of this phase is influenced by a multitude of factors. One thing is for sure, no matter how positively a career starts, eventually one's initial optimism will be in some ways diminished over time. This isn't completely negative. Having a dose of reality and evolution of perspective can be beneficial to the execution of work. Conversely, at an extreme, one may become cynical about the work and the people. Somewhere short of that response, one might simply execute one's work with a steadfast desolation largely devoid of any positive emotional investment. Such an approach is arguably efficient in terms of daily work execution; however, for those inhabiting such an approach to work, it can become tedious and dull. Harkening back to a Beatnik term, one might say such individuals become *squares* (i.e., individuals who are uptight, boring, or otherwise no fun to be around). It is worth stating explicitly that *something* can occur in the enactment of work which over time moves people from a position of gratitude to one of resignation. People's zest for work, career, or life more broadly becomes diminished over their career. Approaching this situation metaphorically may provide a useful starting point for understanding and examining it more concretely.

Unpacking complexity is aided by distinguishing between what is known, what is familiar, what is novel, and what is unknown. When attempting to make sense of complex phenomena which are novel or unknown, metaphors are helpful. As explained by Lakoff and Johnson (2003), "our ordinary conceptual system, in terms of which we both think and act, is fundamentally metaphorical in nature" (p. 3), and that "the essence of metaphor is understanding and experiencing one kind of thing in terms of another" (p. 5). Some likely unfamiliar ground has been covered regarding management as an ideology and how one's view towards work and self is transformed vis-à-vis its organizational enactment. Starting with the metaphor of water, we can attempt to make sense of this observable aspect of work. One characteristic of water is that without a fixed shape, water conforms to the shape of the container which surrounds it. Keeping this mind, one might note that the human body is comprised of up to 60% water. Consequently, it should be no surprise that humans at work, when constrained to cubicles, tend to become squares. The following piece of détournement explores this phenomenon artistically.

Squares in Cubes

Through an expansive emptiness, a sense of desolation is captured in the détournement, *Squares in Cubes*. The long pathway along the openings of the cubicles is occasionally interrupted by an outpouring of squares. These squares symbolize colleagues *hanging out* and chatting. The "No Circles" sign, prominently displayed in the front cubicle, reflects a meager attempt to personalize one's cube. Its oblique allusion can be seen as an attempt to convince oneself (or others) through an exclusion of circles, that one wants to project being happy in one's squareness as well as *those circle-types* not being welcome in the space. Is it purely by chance that privacy is offered only to those who spend their days crouching? After years of inhabiting such a space, it is not surprising many look for some means of improvement perhaps in the form of escape. This is certainly understandable if one wants out or if one wants privacy. The half-sized walls of the cubicles make them ideal for the penetrating gaze of those in charge who stand upright in the corridor and manage by walking around. This ever-present threat of managerial observation is an important aspect of organizational power. Ideally, this détournement communicates a feeling of isolation as one sits alone surrounded by others in an empty office void. With this dynamic well-established, attention can be drawn to organizational power and its consequences on individual workers.

In an examination of organizational power, it is useful to start with a reflection on the individual. In terms of work, a given individual goes to a building (or increasingly logs in virtually) and subsequently interacts with colleagues and management. When envisioned thusly, it is easy to reduce *organizational power* to the direct interactions between the individual and management. Such a construction, while logical, misses generative dynamics between organizational power, management, and the individual. Foucault (1980) described that, "the individual is not a pre-given entity which is seized on by the exercise of power. The individual, with his identity and characteristics, is the product of a relation of power" (pp. 73-74), and further, "the individual is an effect of power, and at the same time, or precisely to the extent to which it is that effect, it is the element of its articulation. The individual which power has constituted is at the same time its vehicle"

(p. 98). Within this framework an *individual* within an office is an outcome of a regime of organizational power. This transformation was alluded to in the détournement, *Squares in Cubes*, in which something outside the individual contributes to what that individual becomes through the processes of working. The *square* one might become at work can be viewed as a metaphoric example of Foucault's individual as a "product of a relation of power." Examining organizational power further will reveal more underlying and contributing to this dynamic.

In an examination of organizational power, it is important to delimit what is meant by *organization* and *power.* Analyzing the term organization, an *organization* is here any entity comprised of numerous individuals who are engaged in hierarchical, collective action in which pay is earned through the execution of directed work within a professional, office setting (physical or virtual). Some of the key aspects of an organization as defined are, *individuals*, *collective actions*, *hierarchies*, *directed work*, *profession*, and *compensation*. Given that the term organization is modifying the term power in the phrase organizational power, the provided definitional delimitation of the concept *organization* is considered at least minimally sufficient for the purpose of this critique. While both terms are important, *power* is considered more consequential in its ultimate effect. As such, a little more rigor is given to the parameters of its definition and delimitation. To start, both power and organization are foundational to human activity and accomplishment. As such it is worthy of study. Green (2013) explained:

> Power is an inexorable force carving directions out of the fabric of evolution. Present at every level of manifestation, it poses particular challenges for a socially adapted species such as humans. Power, as a primal flow, and organization,

> as a primal act, are both present at every moment of our lives within multiple different contexts. With this understanding, power and organization become vital places of inquiry and targets for conscious evolution. (p. 102)

Power, as indicated by Green, is problematic. It produces *challenges* for humans across a variety of contexts including organizations. Confronting, and ideally overcoming, these challenges is beneficial to those seeking greater authenticity and autonomy at work. Pfeffer (1992) defined *power* as "the potential ability to influence behavior, to change the course of events, to overcome resistance, and to get people to do things that they would not otherwise do," and further that "politics and influence are the processes, the actions, the behaviors through which this potential power is utilized and realized" (p. 45). Central to Pfeffer's construction of power is *coercion*. Pfeffer provided a view of power as the mechanism by which people are compelled to do what they otherwise would not. This construction is useful in an organizational sense. As previously indicated, an organization can be either physical or virtual. Power, therefore; must be able to transverse geographic, cyber, and functional distances to be operational within an organizational sense. In addressing a unified conception of organizational power, Bartley, Soener, and Gershenson (2019) argued that "organizational power is increasingly exercised at a distance – not only geographically but also in the sense of being mediated by multiple organizational boundaries and technologies of valuation" (p. 2).

Collectively, this review of organizational power suggests that organizations are sites in which power is enacted. This can be direct or indirect, proximate or distant, and compels workers within institutions to perform activities (i.e., do things) they wouldn't otherwise do. Green's work suggests that power in organizations, while consequential, is open to adaption. An alternative to the current construction of management as an ideology is developed more fully in section five (*a path forward*) of this book. With this notion of organizational power developed, one can examine aspects of organizational power dynamics.

Power is enacted through a network of interconnected channels in dynamic exchanges throughout organizations. Given a global economy where multinational corporations engage in multi-echelon business operations with subsidiaries and suppliers around the world, this interconnected web of dynamic exchanges becomes increasingly complex and multidimensional. The particular power dynamics at play within a given organization, at a particular moment in time, are as consequential as they are unique. In general, an organization's power dynamics can influence what gets done (or doesn't get done), how the work gets done (in terms of task prioritization and execution approach), who gets recognized (or excluded from recognition) for the work, as well as how the work gets discussed, interpreted, and eventually institutionally archived (i.e., its official rhetorical contextualization). In an examination of organizational power, Kras, Portillo, and Taxman (2017) found that, "power dynamics" exist within organizations, and they "have the potential to shape the ways in which policies are ultimately enacted" (p. 216). Whereas power dynamics are consequential organizationally, open discussions about organizational power and power dynamics are conspicuously absent. When the topics of organizational power and power dynamics are discussed, they frequently occur using vague platitudes related to notions of *empowerment*. Why might this be? One reason for this might be that while generalized attributes exist, organizational power is manifest in specific ways and contexts. Another reason might be that it is inherently awkward due to power asymmetries between those wielding power and those subjugated to it to engage in an open discussion of its application. A more critical reason is likely that referencing organizational power directly brings it into focus. To identify and vocalize that organizational power exists will eventually lead to it being called into question. For this reason, those who use organizational power or benefit from its use, likely attempt to obfuscate it. This is facilitated, as was presented earlier, through the theory and praxis of management as an ideology. This lack of awareness is consequential to the individuals engaged directly in work execution, as it potentially affects both organizational performance and existential well-being. As a result, the concern is both pragmatically and ethically important, as it has both operational and human consequences.

A generalized understanding of organizational power is useful for establishing its broad contours. Assessing and understanding organizational power *in action* necessitates an examination of a specific instance surrounding its use. Elements of time, place, and participants factor into understanding a particular manifestation of organizational power. Willmott (2013) explained, "our knowledge of power cannot be extracted from the particular relations of power (e.g., the epistemic community) through which its sense is articulated and justified...conceptions of power are therefore pregnant with political and ethical significance" (p. 285). While specific analyses of organizational power are outside the focus of this critique, it is essential to appreciate the limitation produced through its absence. Two areas in which a generalized understanding of organizational power falls short are the constraints workers face within an organization and the justifications used by management to legitimate power (if/when any are given). Berti and Simpson (2021) explained that "power relations can constrict organizational members' capacities for coping with contradictions, while inhibiting the possibility for signaling the absurdity of their condition to decision-makers" (p. 258). Tasks are sometimes contradictory. At a minimum, tasks can sometimes appear to be contradictory to those executing work with incomplete information. The ability to voice the perceived absurdities associated with a given task is important for figuring out its purpose as well as if the task needs to be accomplished at all, or if a lower-quality submission is adequate given the relative value of the task. A feeling of absurdity often reveals work which doesn't require too much (or any) investment. It is difficult to figure this out if one is unable to discuss these suspicions. Management as an ideology suggests that all tasks are important, and each requires one's best effort. Neither of which is *true*. Furthermore, even if it were true and all tasks are important and warrant one's best effort, constraints of time make executing that vision impossible to enact. When forced to do so, workers experience both *subjugation* (i.e., being brought under organizational control) and *alienation* (i.e., estrangement from one's work). Much could be said about worker subjugation and alienation. Since the focus of this critique is on management in quandary, worker subjugation and alienation are only mentioned in passing. Not because it is unimportant, but simply because it is largely obvious and well documented. The second concern identified focuses on the justifications of organizational power. Understanding how a conceptualization of power is justified regarding its conditions and consequences is essential (Willmott). Again, there is no generalizable justification for the use of organizational power, only the generalized insight that the justification for its use is frequently implicit or vaguely established within management as an ideology. Ideally, addressing the general attributes of organizational power will allow for its subsequent identification, confrontation, and overcoming of the specific instances observed at work. Establishing greater authenticity and autonomy at work requires a novel response to existing patterns of organizational power.

In thinking about the networks of organizational power that are enacted through management as an ideology, it is helpful to start with an examination of the individual. While one can never know *a priori* what any given individual will do, it is possible to observe patterns associated with groups of individuals and ascertain what they tend to do on average. That information provides some insight into activities, decisions, and approaches, which are relatively more or less probable. Making use of observational data is inherently problematic. One issue associated with observational data is that the person who makes the observations could do so poorly, inaccurately, or with bias (intentional or unintentional). Another issue associated with observational data is one could confuse cause and effect or misattribute the direction of causality. Additionally, among the factors being observed, there could be multicollinearity, or the behavior being observed could be too complex to understand through simple observation. Lastly, given the time horizon over which careers are enacted there is ample room for feedback loops between cause and effect which would make untangling foundational dynamics nearly impossible through observation. Collectively, these issues suggest that one should be cautious when formulating understandings based on observations. With this caveat in mind, it is still useful, at least for purposes of conceptualization, to explore observations for potentially useful insights.

Observationally, there is a perception that individuals choose one of two distinct career paths. Through a series of internal inclinations and external enticements, one tends to either pursue a career path related to technical excellence (i.e., a specialist) or one related to broad operational competence over diverse functional areas (i.e., a generalist). Either of these two career paths can lead to personal fulfillment, self-respect, and social esteem. While neither path is inherently *better* than the other, there are differences which a worker benefits from understanding and considering strategically. As the name implies, a *specialist* has a narrower path of advancement. Since the selected area of expertise is *specialized* (which organizationally implies atypical), there will be fewer positions in general for a specialist, and certainly much fewer higher-paid positions. While the path of advancement is narrower, being a technical expert provides greater space for authenticity and autonomy that is nearly always absent from the generalist path. Since one is recognized as *a* technical expert (perhaps *the* technical expert) within an organization, one can do what one wants (in terms of the application of one's specialized knowledge), the way one wants to do it, without anybody within the organization being able to question it. Additionally, one is routinely included in senior-level discussions and when one's input is sought, it is nearly always taken into serious consideration even if it is not always followed. For those in professions (e.g., accountancy, analytics, engineering), being a senior technical expert is often rewarding and fulfilling position; however, there are at least two other elements to consider, pay and prestige.

As discussed, at the culmination of the specialist career path, a technical expert obtains a degree of authenticity and autonomy within the organization. At the highest level, a technical expert will almost always make more money and have more prestige within the organization than that of the lower-echelon, general manager; however, there is a limit as to how far a technical expert will progress within the organization. In terms of pay, a technical expert will likely earn somewhere between the salary of an upper, mid-level or lower, upper-level manager, which generally equates to a rather significant wage. Even with this, there is always the potential enticement of *more*. Additionally, assuming the technical expert is completely unencumbered by supervisory responsibility, the generalist path has a degree of power associated with having directional authority over a pool of subordinates. The incentive structure of organizations routinely privileges the generalist path over that of the specialist. The technical expert eventually reaches a point at which it is clear one will not advance further (within the technical field) and one's earning potential is diminished. At that point, the only advancement possible within the organization is to transition into management. Doing so likely requires sacrificing some of the authenticity and autonomy gained through technical expertise and experiencing the subjugation and alienation of generalists and lower echelon managers.

The path of the generalist is more consistent in its focus and content. A generalist becomes proficient in the execution of work within an organization. Central to this proficiency is an understanding of what information is needed from whom and how to coordinate that information for effective task closure. In short, one learns how to get things done within an organization. Unlike the technical expert, the generalist's focus is on understanding the people and processes of the organization. Knowing who can say no and grind the effort to a halt is a key piece of information. Being an effective generalist requires one to understand people. This isn't people in general, but specific people holding specific positions within the organization. It also requires one to know something about each function within the organization. Among the generalist's primary skills are the ability to synthesize across functions, integrate and coordinate information, and bring tasks to closure. Since generalists advance through the organization based on dutifully executing organizational directives and conforming to organizational expectations a generalist is immediately and always subjugated and potentially alienated. Again, in contrast to a technical expert, there isn't much advancement potential for a nonsupervisory generalist (i.e., a generalist who is not a manager). The highest organizational level a generalist is likely to achieve outside of management is a midlevel position. However, through the management path, a generalist frequently gains access for advancement to the highest echelons available within an organization. Like the technical expert, there are structural-organizational constraints which incentivize the career generalist towards management. Whether it is pay, prestige, or simply the competitiveness associated with *winning*, both the technical expert and the generalist will reach a point at which the question becomes, is one's career (in terms of advancement) over or will one pursue a managerial position. Since alternative constructions are theoretically available, one must conclude such a structural inevitability is by design. Having a replenishing pool of workers who think they want to pursue positions of management is certainly advantageous for organizational executives.

Since management as an ideology obfuscates organizational power from the individual, one might be largely unaware of the extent to which one's career outlook and goals have been shaped institutionally. As with any ideology, there is the potential for false consciousness. There is little doubt that those in control have preferences as to what is desirable in an employee. As Bartley, Soener, and Gershenson (2019) explained, "within organizational boundaries, executives and managers work to shape the behavior and outlook of employees, producing their image of the 'ideal worker'" (p. 3). Such an "ideal worker" might be *productive*, *positive*, *punctual*, *knowledgeable*, *collaborative*, or any number (or combination) of admirable and beneficial qualities. Desiring to advance through the managerial ranks is likely part of what an organization wants to see in its workforce. On the list of desirable attributes of an employee, seldom would the quality *authentic* make an executive's list of characteristics associated with the ideal worker. Almost never would *autonomous* be desired, unless it is being advocated for in its narrowest sense, meaning one is able to work effectively remotely.

In this section, the concept of management as an ideology was presented. From this starting point, the position was developed that management as an ideology contains the systematic error or false consciousness resident in ideologies (Althusser, 2014; Sloterdijk, 1987; Žižek, 2009). Further, the work of Deem and Brehony (2005) established that one could consider management as an ideology to be widespread and existing as a form of legitimization. The détournement, *Squares in Cubes*, illustrated the isolation and exposure associated with working in modernity. As a result, these points addressed the dynamics of organizational power. Lastly, the structural funneling which incentivizes workers to consider moving into management was discussed. For many, once they make that determination, they advance forward (and upward) under the banner of the age-old battle cry, *if you can't beat them, join them*. This advancing march often embodies a hope to make things better. As discussed, both technical experts and career generalists might find the attempt to advance (escape) into management too seductive to ignore. An exploration as to what they might find when they do is presented in the following section.

Key Concepts

- Alienation
- Authenticity
- Autonomy
- Management as an ideology
- Organizational power
- Subjugation

Reflection Questions

1. Reflect on your current or previous work experiences. In your reflection call to mind what you did, how you did it, and with whom you interacted. What aspects of the work were ennobling? What aspects of the work were demeaning?
2. Given the experiences described in response to question one, what things could you have done to make your work more ennobling and less demeaning? What could your manager have done to make the work experience more positive?
3. Often people are excited to start a new career, only to find that with time their initial enthusiasm wanes. In what ways has your employment made you more interesting and alive as an individual? In what ways has it diminished your vigor and joy for being who you are? What could you do to make work a place in which you become more dynamic?
4. What are some of the key elements associated with ideologies? In what ways is management an ideology? To what degree do your experiences of working align with an ideological construction of management?

5. Create an x-axis that goes from alienated on the left side to authentic on the right side. Likewise, create a y-axis that goes from subjugated at the bottom to autonomous at the top. Using this coordinate map place dots where they most closely capture your different employment contexts (this isn't an exact science, approximations are encouraged). Now place a diamond where you would like to be in the future. How close or far is your desired location from your previous locations? What does this suggest?
6. Write a paragraph describing your thoughts when you read the phrase *organizational power*. To what degree are your views of organizational power positive, negative, or neutral? As you reflect on your response, was it informed primarily from the perspective of being a manager or from being a subordinate? In what way would your response change if you favored the alternative perspective?

II. The Unbearable Banality of Management

Wishing is the joy
Eventually fulfilled
Consistently dark

Vaunted for is prestige and power the allure of management is seductive. As indicated in part one, *squares in cubes*, whereas work in theory holds the potential for self-expression and accomplishment, often it seems plagued by monotonous drudgery and conformity in practice. Confronting the unrelenting pressures of work, it is understandable that one might look hopefully to management as the most available and immediate means of improving one's situation as well as to make a difference in the organization. Frequently, advancing into management brings with it increases in salary and status. Additionally, one often holds the implicit assumption that because management has the accepted authority of *control*, that once in that position, one will be able to have greater autonomy, if not also authenticity, at work. One will eventually find that is seldom the case; however, especially initially, attaining a managerial position seems to deliver on its promise. As alluded to in the opening haiku for this section, one should be careful when making wishes. Over an extended period of a career, darker aspects of being a manager can appear. Only two of these darker elements will be discussed, *alienation* and *despair.* When alienation is discussed in terms of economics, it is often discussed in terms of workers being alienated from the product of one's labor. This is certainly the traditional Marxian usage of alienation. In this critique of organizational power, the concept of subjugation is applied equally to workers and lower-echelon managers. For management, the alienation principally addressed is the alienation from *oneself,* which emerges when a manager must adhere to and parrot corporate positions. These can be inconsistent with one's views. When this occurs frequently, in conjunction with previous promotions to higher echelons of management and diminished prospects for further advancement, a manager can transition from a state of alienation to a state of despair. Such a situation not only affects the manager, but it also impacts those being managed. Placing the elements of *alienation* and *despair* in context is facilitated by a cursory review of some key aspects of established, mainstream management theory which allude to these concerns.

As indicated in section one, *squares in cubes,* the topic of management is extensively studied but known only incompletely. Studies referenced in that section pertained to largely positive themes residing at the core of management as an ideology. CMS was presented as a domain which critiques the assumptions and structural foundations of traditional constructions of management theory and praxis. Critiques of management can be found in more mainstream research as well. Studies focused on concerning aspects of management include understaffing (Halldorsdottir, Einarsdottir &

Edvardsson, 2018; Martin, 2015; Welch, Williams, Darville, Smartt & McBroom, 2015), inadequate support (Middaugh, 2018; Westgate, Musoke, Crigler & Perry, 2021), lack of communication (Murphy & Poist, 1992; Rahim, 2011), skepticism (Terpstra & Rozell, 1998), cynicism (Demirci, 2019; Pfrombeck, Doden, Grote & Feierabend, 2020; Pugh, Skarlicki & Passell, 2003), and dissatisfaction (Morrison, Oladunjoye & Onyefulu, 2007; Reineholm, Gustavsson, Liljegren & Ekberg, 2012). The issue is not so much that critiques of management are nonexistent (as they clearly exist in a variety of forms and foci), but rather that those learning about managerial theory and enacting management in praxis are exposed inadequately to the insights of these critiques prior to being confronted with the organizational realities obfuscated by management as an ideology (if they become aware of these perspectives at all). Examinations and critiques of the deleterious consequences of management seldom escape the inner sanctum of the ivory tower of academia. It is certainly worth every attempt to bridge this gap between those conducting research about management and those living it directly, as it is one way to prepare better those aspiring for managerial positions for what they will eventually face and experience.

Before further exploring the topic of management, it is essential to establish a shared definition and understanding of its theory and praxis. In short, the ideological essence of management needs to be defined. At a minimum, key aspects of management should be sketched out, at least provisionally. So, what is management? And what is it that managers do? As explained in the preface, management is frequently presented as the discipline focused on accomplishing tasks and achieving goals using the planning, organizing, staffing, directing, and controlling functions, processes, and resources within an organization. Whereas this is useful as a starting point, one should take care when dealing with the theory and praxis of management to avoid reductionist constructs. Management is complex. Managers are not simply one thing. In fact, Mintzberg (1971) established that managers perform ten basic roles within organizations. Discussing each of these ten roles is beyond the scope of this critique. One of the key roles; however, is worthy of explicit development. The management role of *nerve center* identified by Mintzberg highlights the specialist/generalist dynamic presented in section one, *squares in cubes*. As described by Mintzberg, managers can function as the "nerve center of internal information," and that while the manager "may not know as much about any one function as the subordinate who specializes in it," the manager "comes to know more about his total organization than any other member. He is the information generalist" (p. B-104). Such a situation places managers in a somewhat precarious situation. While one is administratively superior to one's subordinates, the subordinates can, and often do, have greater technical knowledge. This could influence the way decision making is enacted by management. In terms of organizational decision making, Lindblom (1959) explained, "decision-making is ordinarily formalized as a means-ends relationship: means are conceived to be evaluated and chosen in the light of ends finally selected independently and prior to the choice of means...such a means-ends relationship is possible only to the extent that values are agreed upon, and reconcilable, and are stable at the margin" (p. 83); in the absence of these characteristics, managers benefit from an approach of "muddling through" (p. 88). Again, this places managers in a rather precarious situation as the *means*, *ends*, *goals*, and *priorities* are being simultaneously defined and enacted. Thus far, the task of management has been found to be precarious insofar as one's subordinates potentially have more granular knowledge than the manager and the decision-making process is *muddled*. Additionally, the task of management itself might be overwhelming. As Mintzberg explained within management, "the quantity of work is great; the pace is unrelenting; there is great variety, fragmentation, and brevity in the work activities; the manager must concentrate on issues that are current, specific, and ad hoc" (p. B-108). Once the initial excitement of becoming a manager has subsided and the novelty of the pay increase has diminished, one is often forced to confront the inherent challenges of management, which are presented inadequately in college textbooks and office discussions. At this point, one is forced to confront what management as an ideology has successfully obfuscated.

In larger organizations, management exists at multiple echelons. As previously mentioned, often when one is a manager, one is also still a subordinate. In other words, managers have managers. When an organizational structure like this occurs, all the issues associated with dealing with management as an ideology covered in section one, *squares in cubes*, reside at the managerial level as well. In fact, it is not infrequent for a second-level manager (i.e., a manager of managers) to have fewer subordinate managers than a first-level manager who has subordinate workers. What does this mean? It means that a second-level manager can give even more oversight to a first-level manager than a first-level manager is able to give to subordinate workers. So, if one was motivated to become a manager to escape the *gaze* of management, this move could backfire as one might end up getting even more attention as a manager than one did as a subordinate. When this occurs, it could be a shocking irony for the unsuspecting manager. This topic is developed more fully in part three, *the spectacle of work*. Something like this situation exists if one thought that becoming a manager would mean one gained more autonomy in the process. Again, since a first-level manager is still subordinate to a second-level manager (i.e., a manager residing at the next-higher organizational echelon), that second-level manager will scope the workload of the first-level manager. One might find that situation is worse than it was as a worker insofar as when one was a worker the assignments, directions, and goals were at least clear. As a manager, each of these things can be vague, which creates additional stress due to expectation ambiguities. In terms of both scrutiny and direction, the manager hasn't escaped the drudgery experienced as a worker; rather, one simply finds oneself in a more complex, nebulous version of the same organizational dynamics. Managers finding themselves in such a situation are no less subjugated by organizational power than their subordinates, which can produce a feeling of being trapped in the middle. In addition to this subjugation, managers might experience increased alienation. This potential alienation is multidimensional and can lead to despair.

The alienation managers potentially experience is different in both degree and type from that experienced by those at the working level within organizations. Workers, as described in section one, *squares in cubes*, are routinely alienated from the product of their labor. Managers, as subordinates to higher-echelon managers are as well; however, given the extent of managerial tasks, this alienation likely has a wider scope. In terms of type, since managers are the *embodiment* and *voice* of corporate positions, they are potentially alienated from themselves. This point will be developed further subsequently. Regarding external relationships, management is *isolating* and associations for managers are *estranged*. From below, managers are discouraged from being social with their subordinates. When a manager is quasi-social with one's subordinates, it is difficult for the manager to know if the interaction is based on the position or one's personality. Further, perceived friendships with subordinates can complicate the execution of work. At the level of one's peers within the organization, managers are guarded with their colleagues as they are the people with whom they are in direct competition for opportunities, advancement, and promotion. From above, managers attempt to project competence and impress those for whom they work. Often managers try to please their supervisors and those holding higher positions within the organization. Managers are surrounded by alienation at work. Whether from above, across, or below, managers limit how much of themselves they share with others. Management forms an inherent barrier to authenticity. Sharing too much with subordinates can blur the line between official and personal relationships. Divulging too much with peers can provide them with an advantage in the office politics of competition for advancement. Revealing too much with one's superiors can convey that one doesn't understand the system or make one appear indiscreet. When a manager assesses this situation objectively, rationality dictates against authenticity. Pursuing authenticity exposes one to risks without much potential gain. Consequently, managers become depersonalized functionaries of the organization. This estrangement is compounded by the fact that managers also face potential alienation from themselves as they present corporate positions to their subordinates.

When contrary to one's personal view, giving voice to corporate positions holds the potential to alienate a manager not only from others, but more problematically from oneself. This is an aspect of management which is both complex and subtle. Whereas this task is discussed openly as a legitimate function of management, the alienation which ensues as a consequence is obfuscated by management as an ideology. When there is an incongruity between the corporate view and one's personal view, managers are, as organizational functionaries, required to administer the *party line* (i.e., the view espoused by higher-echelon, corporate managers). Not only are managers required to present the corporate view, but they are obligated to do so as if the corporate position was their own. Such an action requires a manager to subordinate one's thoughts and feelings to the will of the organization as asserted by those at an upper echelon. This dynamic betrays that managers as well as workers are subjugated by the organizational power resident in management as an ideology. Again, the reality that managers are required to do this is presented as part of management theory and praxis. Mintzberg (1971) referred to this role of management as the *disseminator*, noting that, "here, the manager acts as the mechanism by which organizational influencers (owners... the 'boss') make their preferences known to the organization. It is the manager's duty to....express general organizational preferences" (p. B-105). Omitted from the discussion is how a manager experiences this subjugation and alienation when the corporate view is inconsistent with one's own. To use a piece of throwback slang, it is difficult to imagine how a manager could enact this without feeling like a *hack* (i.e., a person who works obediently and at a level of mediocre quality). Why would a manager be willing to sacrifice one's personal views for those of the organization? The shortest and most direct answer is because such an action is consistent with management as an ideology. At a more descriptive level, when managers present a corporate view with which they disagree as if it were their own, they do so to either keep their current job or to be considered a strong candidate for future advancement (i.e., promotion) within the organization. This aspect of management forms a nexus of economic, psychological, sociological, and philosophical concerns. Whereas one might argue the ethical, organizational, personal, and financial costs and benefits associated with a manager's willingness to subordinate themselves to organizational demands pragmatically, one benefits from understanding that for managers there are decreasing opportunities.

There is certainly an allure to infinite possibility. When one feels like one can accomplish anything, work is approached with inspired creativity. The converse is structurally offsetting. When one feels trapped, one can become stifled and moribund. The shape of the organizational hierarchy can influence the probabilities of these outcomes. This is an important aspect in the critique of organizational power because management as an ideology entices people to pursue a path of advancement. Organizations are structured more like pyramids than squares. There are a multitude of positions at the bottom (i.e., at the worker level), fewer positions in the middle (i.e., at the technical expert or managerial level), and only a handful of positions at the top (i.e., the executive level). Consequently, as one advances in one's career there is less lateral space to the sides and even less space above. What does this mean in practice? Literally, it means that as one is promoted within an organization, there are decreasing opportunities for advancement or transfer. When this occurs, one experiences a feeling of being *stuck*. Perhaps one will experience a corresponding feeling of anxiety and panic or despair. At this point in their career, managers are often at a loss as to what to do, especially if they have considerable time before retirement. They have invested themselves into an organization and no longer see a viable path forward. This is the point at which things obfuscated by management as an ideology are experienced directly, but without an explicit framework for understanding. Since it would be *inappropriate* for a manager to discuss this with one's subordinates, *risky* to discuss it with one's peers, and *limiting* to discuss it with one's superiors, managers frequently suffer in silence. Such an outcome can lead to despair. This structural isolation is not accidental but is a consequence of management as an ideology. It is useful to step back and reflect on the structural dynamics which contributed to this outcome.

When one was working (either as a technical specialist or a career generalist), the path of management seemed like a viable path forward (and upward) to gain authenticity and autonomy at work. One likely envisioned that becoming a manager would lead to being in charge, directing organizational activity, and inspiring subordinates. What one discovers is that managers are often engaged in the *mundane, trivial, petty* problems between subordinates and customers. Rather than being involved in activities of organizational consequence, one finds oneself entrapped by persistent banality and irrelevance. While moving up the corporate ladder, one also moves away; vertical distance emerges between the manager and the managed and lateral distance increases between the manager and one's peers often resulting in a sense of isolation. The following piece of détournement provides a point of reflection.

The Unbearable Banality of Management

II. The Unbearable Banality of Management

Few things are as trivially irksome within an organization as inspirational posters. Such posters become visible focal points for the chasm existing between corporate managers and those engaged in work. As those in corporate imagine these trite images are motivating, the workers mock every aspect of them. One can imagine a corporate poster showing up one day in common workspace or a manager being directed to spruce up the workspace to inspire the workforce. In any event, the *Hang in There!* poster appears against a black void. Businesses appear to be the cosmic repository for the accumulation of motivational posters. An edgy response can act as a counterbalance to such *motivation* and becomes a single piece of authenticity for the manager. However, there are two things to note. First, the framed print of muted rebellion faces the manager, so others are unable to see it. Second, the manager's slogan of sedition, *read between the lines*, is playful rather than assertive. These two aspects combine to reveal a manager who is afraid to declare one's thought openly and forcefully. The détournement, *The Unbearable Banality of Management*, captures a sense of isolation along with management's meager attempt for a personal message of humor and resistance to provide sustenance in one's despair. As a means to review and solidify the main point , the predicament in which managers find themselves might be explained beneficially using statistics as a metaphor.

Borrowing a concept from statistics might be constructive for understanding the possible alienation and despair while advancing through the managerial echelons. In statistics, *degrees of freedom* are the number of values which can vary within a calculation while obtaining the same result. The higher the degrees of freedom, the more latitude which exists. Typically, advancing in one's career through the ranks of management is viewed positively. One generally makes more money and has more status. Assuming this is common enough that it can be generally accepted, management as an ideology obfuscates subtle negatives which lurk behind these espoused positives. Few people consider these aspects until they find themselves long-established in managerial positions. At which point it feels like it is too late; one feels trapped. Prior to starting a career, it can feel that the possibilities are endless. In fact, there can be a degree of randomness associated with the industry in which one is initially employed since entry-level jobs typically do not require substantial experience and are designed to develop the individual. As one advances; however, skills and knowledge become increasingly specialized. This makes it challenging to move to another industry. Even when this isn't technically accurate, industries can be exceedingly parochial, eschewing those from outside the narrow pedigree those in control view as essential. Further, as previously discussed, as one is promoted, there are fewer jobs at or above that given level. Lastly, as one is promoted and finds that one's situation is appreciably the same in terms of personal fulfillment, there is decreasing hope that the next promotion will make life appreciably *better* existentially. Consequently, for every step up a corporate ladder, there are fewer steps above, fewer viable, lateral opportunities, and less hope about the transformational potential associated with advancement. A sense of being trapped and feelings of despair are not uncommon.

Of all the aspects obfuscated by management as an ideology, perhaps the most consequential existentially is the alienation experienced by managers. Because this aspect is so well hidden in standard treatments of management, it becomes an important area of focus in this critique of organizational power. As indicated previously, a concern for *alienation* in labor relations is quintessentially Marxian. Shantz, Alfes, and Truss (2014) explained, "the idea of work alienation has a very long history...Marx conceptualized alienation as the separation of a worker from the product that was created, the process by which it was created, or from others who are involved in the production or consumption of the product" (p. 2530). Insofar as this work is focused on the concern of *workplace alienation*, the critique of organizational power discussed could be considered *Marxian*. However, since the alternative proposed in section five of this book, *a path forward*, suggests only modifications to how the functions of management are enacted organizationally and not the abandonment or radical overthrowing of the structural basis of free-market capitalism, it would be incorrect to categorize this critique as *Marxist*. It clearly is not. The contextual gap between *Marxian* and *Marxist*, might at first seem to be an academic distinction without a pragmatic difference. In fact, the difference between the two constructions, while subtle, is both essential and consequential. The following quip is useful as a starting point for understanding the distinction. *Just because Marx was wrong about communism, doesn't mean he was also wrong about capitalism*. The point conveyed using this statement and the philosophical stance staked in this work is that Marx identified an important shortcoming of capitalism when he noted its propensity for engendering alienation. Marx's proposed solution to that problem was communism. This critique of organizational power is consistent with Marx's diagnosis of the problem, which is alienation (i.e., *Marxian*), but rejects Marx's prognosis of the solution, which is communism (i.e., *Marxist*). Whereas Marxian critiques of management are rare, some studies are suggesting burgeoning interest in its application (Shantz, Alfes, &Truss).

Addressing the alienation and subsequent despair of managers benefits from situating the context in which it might emerge and those factors which contribute to its potential emergence. Numerous factors play into the degree to which a manager might experience alienation. Notions such as *pride*, *dignity*, and *empowerment* benefit from being analyzed in terms of their respective contribution. Whereas organizational power is obfuscated by management as an ideology, the degree of power exerted throughout the organization is a likely contributing factor to alienation. As Hodson noted (1996) "high management power, based on rule by fiat, creates an absence of mutually agreed upon norms that have currency with workers. This type of workplace is associated with low pride and reduced dignity for workers. Such workplaces can be based on direct supervision, assembly-line technology, or bureaucracy. All three of these organizations of work undermine positive task-related and coworker-related aspects of work" (p. 735). The work of Hodson provides some useful insights related to workplace alienation. First, when organizational rules and regulations are highly dictatorial in nature, this prohibits the formulation of organic and authentic norms of behavior. Second, an absence of the inherent pride or dignity associated with the work itself can contribute to a sense of alienation. As stated previously, all jobs and tasks have inherent dignity. The way organizations enact that work or treat the people enacting the work can either bolster or diminish that inherent dignity. When tasks and positions are diminished, the feeling of alienation is more likely to occur. This has implications for managers via the transitive property since overseeing work which is maligned organizationally has a compounding effect for those managing that work. Lastly, the organizational structure itself contributes to alienation. As Hodson indicated, organizations making use of direct supervision and bureaucratic structures are particularly susceptible to alienation. It is at this point specifically that the alienation of managers becomes clear. Management is the *sine qua non* of direct supervision and bureaucracy. These are the organizational structures built on cascading networks of hierarchical management. As such, managers and workers alike in these organizations confront the structural source of organizational power and subsequent subjugation and alienation. It is not just the bureaucratic nature of the organizational structure which contributes to the alienation of managers. The workload of managers itself could potentially be a further source of alienation due to the sense of subjugation managers experience when *incentivized* to implement policies inconsistent with their own views or to prioritize workload which is inconsistent with their assessment of its relative value. This source of alienation is worthy of exploration.

Proficiency is gained through repetition. Whereas specialists gain expertise in their respective areas of focus, generalists (and by extension managers) are unable to gain this level of proficiency. As previously indicated, managers become experts at synthesizing information across functional domains to effectively resolve organizational concerns. Such cross-discipline integration can be a source of tension, stress, and alienation for managers. Azambuja and Islam (2019) found that, "as boundary subjects, middle managers...experienced alienation through the ongoing demands for achieving collaboration between divergent interests and for occupying shifting roles. Middle managers sometimes expressed the feeling that such demands were externally driven rather than freely chosen, and diverted them from deepening their professional knowledge and their intimacy with colleagues" (p. 551). The concern related to operating at the boundary of organizations (i.e., integrating across functional areas) has been addressed sufficiently already. However, Azambuja and Islam's research points to another source of alienation, which is the lack of control over priorities This concept warrants subsequent development. The alienation which results from manager's workload being externally driven highlights the importance of *autonomy*. When unable to prioritize work, one becomes estranged from its execution. Such a situation, as indicated by Azambuja and Islam, can create a barrier between the manager and one's subordinates. This finding highlights the importance of *authenticity*. In short, the work of Azambuja and Islam is useful as it highlights that managers can, and do, experience *alienation*, and that *authenticity* and *autonomy* are important to consider in decreasing alienation at work. Given that management as an ideology provides the basis for the execution of organizational power along the channels that contribute to this alienation of managers, it is doubtful that such an outcome is unintentional. If one wants to overcome the subjugation and alienation which is produced by organizational power through management as an ideology, focusing on ways to enhance authenticity and autonomy in organizations is consistent with the research findings of Azambuja and Islam. It is worth noting, that such a concern is not only beneficial existentially to alienated managers, but it is also potentially beneficial in terms of organizational performance due to the centrality of managers in the assignment, execution, and coordination, of work throughout organizations. This concern requires a little more development.

As stated previously, the alienation of managers is different in both degree and type from the alienation experienced by workers. The primary difference is that a manager's alienation has a structurally cascading effect throughout an organization, which is significantly different from that of workers. Of course, workers can, and often do, commiserate with each other, blow off steam, and share their disgruntled feelings. If the degree of alienation amongst the workers is pronounced enough, they might even attempt to bring their collective views to management or to unionize in response. Even at that level, the alienation of management is different. It is different since managers, through the sanctioning of organizational power, are the embodiment and voice of the organization. If a manager is alienated, that sends a different message to the workers than if workers are alienated. While certainly not ideal, management as an ideology acknowledges the prospect of worker alienation. Managers being alienated is contrary to the expectations established through management as an ideology. When managers *go off script,* this can send warning signs that ripple throughout the organization affecting employee performance. As Vanderstukken and Caniels explained, (2021) "supervisors still can and do become alienated from work...when supervisors become alienated, the detrimental consequences for the organization are arguably larger compared with subordinate alienation (given the strong link between supervisor involvement and subordinate performance" (p. 642). The situation of management alienation and despair requires an organizational response. Likely, if upper-echelon managers are aware of the alienation, they might attempt first to council the manager and if that doesn't work, remove the manager. If the manager is removed, it will likely done rhetorically based on substandard subordinate performance. Such a rhetorical justification allows corporate to avoid direct, organizational reference to the issue of management alienation. Management alienation is a concern worthy of being addressed, as it affects the manager, one's subordinates, and organizational performance. Addressing this concern is complicated by the fact that to do so one must identify it as legitimate, which is contrary to management as an ideology. This concern is addressed more fully in section five, *a path forward.* For now, only a few words are provided for context.

Alienation permeates throughout organizations. Workers and managers alike potentially experience its corrosive effects in terms of both organizational performance and existential well-being. Management as an ideology acknowledges worker alienation but obfuscates the alienation of managers. As discussed in section one, *squares in cubes*, workers might attempt escaping alienation by assuming a management position within organizations. This makes the subsequent experiencing of alienation in management even crueler. Addressing this alienation requires a different approach to management as an ideology. As Prasad and Prasad (1993) explained "a reconceptualization of alienation directs management inquiry toward exploring avenues for decommodifying work and human existence, for building community at the workplace, for restoring multidimensionality, and for questioning taken-for-granted assumptions on which contemporary organizations rest" (p. 180). Whereas a response to this concern is developed more fully in section five, *a path forward*, it is important to note that a solution to the concern of alienation is needed. Management as an ideology is failing too many in this respect for its consequences to be ignored. Working with others holds great potential to be ennobling, empowering, and exciting as worthy challenges are overcome and excellence in performance is achieved. Management as an ideology transforms this opportunity for rewarding collegiality into yet another dynamic of organizational power marked by subjugation, alienation, banality, and drudgery. Addressing this concern requires an examination of the system in which it is enacted.

Managers can never be outside the system which legitimates their power and position. They are closer to the organizational core and are increasingly responsible for the enactment of organizational power. Managers are the *embodiment* and *voice* of the organization. Created by, and a consequence of, a regime of organizational power, managers are required to perpetuate the functioning of the *status quo* insofar as it is organizationally beneficial and to implement changes when it is not. Obfuscated by management as an ideology, those who become managers come to experience firsthand that they have no *real* organizational power of their own. They are subordinate functionaries more like those working at the echelon below them than they are like the corporate managers at higher echelons. This is experienced most directly when a gap exists between what corporate managers direct and what a manager thinks and is personally inclined to do. Even if a manager agrees with the corporate position in principle, there are still opportunities for microfractures to exist in terms of temporality (e.g., tell the workforce now/later), style (e.g., use/avoid these certain words in the message), and between the message (i.e., the corporate view) and the medium (i.e., the manager). Metaphorically, a manager is the *dummy* that a corporate ventriloquist operates through the exercise of organizational power. One can never escape the vestiges of organizational power by becoming a manager since one is even more beholding to and part of its functioning. When managers express dissatisfaction with the arrangement, they often receive the dismissive reply, *that is why you are making the big bucks.* Feelings of doubt, shame, and ingratitude can creep into the minds of managers. By internalizing the dissatisfaction and despair, one concludes the problem must be self-inflicted. Through an attempted escape from the drudgery of work, one discovers the banality of management. As the French poet, Jean de La Fontaine explained, *a person often meets his destiny on the road he took to avoid it.* The subjugation and alienation are compounded by the way work is enacted organizationally. Whether as a worker or a manager, knowing that one's work is under observation transforms it into a *spectacle.*

Key Concepts

- Banality
- Despair
- Echelon
- Embodiment
- Generalist
- Muddling through
- Specialist

Reflection Questions

1. List five things associated with becoming a manager that you think will improve the quality of your life. For each element you selected, write one or two sentences explaining how it will make things better. Upon review, what (*if any*) common themes emerge? What does this suggest about your motivations for becoming a manager?
2. Reflect upon a manager for whom you hold a great deal of admiration. What were the characteristics of that individual? Now reflect upon the characteristics you listed. Do you consider these aspects to be largely consistent or inconsistent with the attributes one would expect under management as an ideology? What does this suggest about conforming to or deviating from management as an ideology?
3. Reflect on a manager for whom you have little or no respect. What were the characteristics of that individual? Go through the same reflection on those attributes as you did in question two. What does this suggest about management as an ideology?

4. Terms such as *unbearable*, *banality*, *alienation*, and *despair* figured prominently in section two. These terms tend to have a negative connotation. To what degree has the negative sentiment of these terms nuanced your view of management? To what degree do the positive terms contained in management as an ideology seduce individuals into managerial positions and legitimate its practices?
5. It is commonly known that one cannot serve two bosses. As a manager one is most frequently both a superior and a subordinate. As such, one can identify either up (i.e., towards upper-echelon managers) or down (i.e., towards the ranks from which one came), additionally one can construct one's duty at work as primarily protecting those subordinates under one's charge or enacting the will of one's superiors. There is tension here. With whom will you identify? How will you frame your primary duty?

III. The Spectacle of Work

Seemingly real
Work under a microscope
Endless deception

Organizational power enacted through management as an ideology transforms the way people work. This is the case for managers and subordinates alike. Nobody within the system escapes the judging gaze of superiors. Knowing that the product of one's labor is under organizational scrutiny turns its execution into a *spectacle*. Part of this insight is well established. The fact that employees modify how they execute work in response to observation has been long recognized in business literature. Established with the Hawthorne studies of the 1920s and 1930s, organizational theorists have been aware that observing employees in the process of work is a transformative act. What is less established is how such a situation, especially in larger, bureaucratic organizations, devolves into a *spectacle*. This situation betrays once again one of the common themes developed throughout this critique. The spectacle of work hinders *authenticity* insofar as the enactment of the spectacle constitutes a performance. Further, to adopt elements of pretense in the execution of work is, in-and-of-itself, *alienating*. Additionally, the spectacle of work is predicated upon *subjugation*. If individuals had *autonomy* at work, they would likely pick work they considered to be worthy of personal investment and enact that self-appointed work with passion and zeal. Within the spectacle, it isn't what is being accomplished which matters organizationally; rather, it is what those observing the work being enacted think about its execution (or their assessment as to the perceived quality of what was produced) which is consequential. Essential to the spectacle of work is the degree to which a gap exists between the underlying quality of what is done and how it is assessed organizationally. The larger the gap, the larger the spectacle. Intrinsically, the spectacle of work is the nexus of organizational subjugation and alienation and the fulcrum for greater authenticity and autonomy. Prior to examining the spectacle of work, it is beneficial for context to explore some ancillary topics which are acknowledged in traditional management research. This provides insight into how this topic is treated in management as an ideology.

Traditional management theory recognizes that there are *occasional* issues associated with organizational work. Central to this admission is the simultaneous assertion that such operational *glitches* are incidental to the otherwise smooth functioning of the system. Research related to concerns with work quality has covered an array of areas including inaccuracies and errors (Argyris, 1998; Donovan & Rapp, 2020; Elgammal, Turetken, Heuvel & Papazoglou, 2016), inappropriate behavior (Odermatt, König, Kleinmann, Bachmann, Röder & Schmitz, 2018; Torres, 2005; Wiggins, 2008), and lack of responsiveness (Bohórquez

Arévalo, 2016; Fine, S., & Pirak, 2016; Moeini & Rivard, 2019). Collectively, these elements suggest that the work enacted within organizations is qualitatively different from that which is presented in management as an ideology. These aspects, while critical of facets of organizational work, fall short of the critique made here. Further, traditional management research focuses attention on the individual performing the work rather than the organizational power which shapes, constrains, incentivizes, condones, and ignores the spectacle it plays a part in creating and sustaining. This section addresses the spectacle of work in its immediate and localized manifestation (i.e., the spectacle as it relates to the execution of a single task or project). The long-term consequences of enacting the spectacle of work over an entire career are addressed in section four, *devolving slowly*. To address adequately the spectacle of work, it is important to establish first an element essential for its emergence, *postmodernity*.

The spectacle of work is a postmodern phenomenon. Whereas *postmodern* is difficult to define, and postmodernists would likely resist or contest any singular definitions of what it *is*, there are aspects of postmodernity which can be described. At its core, postmodernity is a rejection of metanarratives (Lyotard, 1984). In practice, a postmodern perspective is critical of claims of universality and instead searches for localized insights and paradoxes. How did this process start and what has been its consequence? Threads of postmodernity are observable in businesses and organizations. As Baudrillard (1994) explained, "it was capital that first fed on the destruction of every referential, of every human objective, that shattered every ideal distinction between true and false, good and evil, in order to establish a radical law of equivalence and exchange, the iron law of its power" (p. 22). Since this is a critique of organizational power, it is useful to connect the insight of

Baudrillard with that of Lyotard regarding how power is operationalized in organizations. As Lyotard explained, "they allocate our lives for the growth of power. In matters of social justice and of scientific truth alike, the legitimation of that power is based on its optimizing the system's performance – efficiency" (p. xxiv). From a postmodern perspective, one of the ways organizational power perpetuates management as an ideology is through the strategic use of language. For Baudrillard "it is the secret of a discourse that is no longer simply ambiguous, as political discourses can be, but that convey the impossibility of a determined position of power, the impossibility of a determined discursive position" (p. 17). As stated previously, management as an ideology obfuscates. Further, the discourse of organizations is prescribed. Those wielding organizational power shape and constrain the types of statements and responses which are acceptable. As Lyotard explained, "constraints function to filter discursive potentials...They...privilege certain classes of statements...whose predominance characterizes the discourse of that...institution: there are things that should be said, and there are...ways of saying them. Thus: orders in the army...questions in philosophy, performativity in business" (p. 17). The postmodern turn suggests much as to the functioning of organizational power exercised through management as an ideology. Consistent with the postmodern perspective, the specific manifestations of organizational power will be unique and localized. Broadly, the postmodern perspective reveals contours as to *how* management as an ideology obfuscates the use of organizational power and that its operationalization is facilitated by its influence over organizational language practices. To contextualize further the spectacle of work, building upon the postmodern perspective presented briefly in this critique, it is useful to examine the notion of the spectacle as originally developed within the Situationist International.

The spectacle of work is a consequence of organizational power enacted through management as an ideology. But what exactly is a spectacle and how does it operate? The construction of the spectacle presented here draws heavily from the work of Debord as he was a founding member of the Situationist International. The Situationist International is an organization that addressed and examined the spectacle in its economic sense. Through theory, a direct linkage between business operations and the spectacle is observable. As Debord explained, "in societies where modern conditions of production prevail, all of life presents itself as an immense accumulation of *spectacles*. Everything that was directly lived has moved away into a representation" (Thesis 1, emphasis in original). This understanding was extended by Debord when he noted "the spectacle, grasped in its totality, is both the result and project of the existing mode of production...as information propaganda, as advertisement...it is the omnipresent affirmation of the choice *already* made in production and its corollary consumption" (Thesis 6, emphasis in original). A key aspect of the spectacle is its replacement of something *real* with an *imitation*. This substitution makes it easier for managers to get the desired response and calls into question what it is that workers are compelled to do if the *actual* and the *artifice* are indistinguishable substitutes. If managers and organizations are no longer constrained by *facts* and instead actively seek substantiating justifications, this propels work further into the realm of spectacle. As described by Jackson (2016), workers attempting to inform "struggle to make their work meaningful to management when the results run counter to that which is desired" (p. 368). This can contribute to a sense of alienation. Such an eventuality reflects a valuation of economics over existentialism and expediency over accuracy. One of the consequences of the spectacle, as developed by Debord, is that once economic considerations (and by extension organizational power) dominate, individual *being* is subordinated to *having*, and subsequently having is subordinated to mere *appearance*. In addition to being a source of alienation, foundations based on appearances are as precarious as they are superficial. Debord identified the spectacle as a source of alienation. This dynamic is obfuscated by management as an ideology and reflects a consequence of organizational power. Workers and managers engaged in the spectacle of work might erroneously think they are engaged in an act of subterfuge or that they are somehow *getting away* with something. While corporate may be unaware of specific acts of the spectacle of work, it is a consequence of the enactment of their organizational power through management as an ideology. When the factual content of a position is null, the available positions are infinite. Such an approach provides those enacting organizational power with limitless flexibility. As Debord explained, "the spectacle is the existing order's uninterrupted discourse about itself, its laudatory monologue. It is the self-portrait of power in the epoch of its totalitarian management of the conditions of existence" (Thesis 24). Within the spectacle of work, one never gets away with anything, even if one is never caught. If those at the upper echelons prefer substantiation over fact and coerce managers and workers to comply, then the spectacle of work can be viewed as another instance of *subjugation*. When enacted by the individual, if the spectacle of work pushes one to privilege appearances over authentic being, then it is *alienating*. Before addressing subjugation and alienation as they relate to the spectacle of work, it is useful to address the performativity required for its organizational enactment.

There is a duality inherent in the concept of performativity as it is described in this critique. The first dealing with language, the second with being. The conceptualization related to language is its more traditional application. Within its linguistics context, *performativity* refers to the ability of language to effect *social* change. In this context, the focus is on how performativity has the capacity to effect *organizational* change. As previously indicated, organizational power shapes and constrains the types of words, phrases, and statements which are permitted (or prohibited). Consequently, organizational power delimits the performativity within organizations. This applies to both managers and subordinates as both groups receive dressage from those at upper echelons regarding appropriate language. It is important to understand this concern is significantly broader than a policy related to workers avoiding the use of *bad words* (which is an absurd construct). More importantly in terms of authenticity and autonomy, the constraints on language through the use of organizational power limit the ability to conceptualize and voice positions which are contrary to management as an ideology. In short, to limit the organizational language is to limit the possibility for debate and dissent. The second way in which performativity is used relates to a person's way of being within the organization. More directly, enacting the spectacle of work is a performance. Individuals adopt the language and a way of being which conveys productivity. In reality, one might be acting. Conducting such a performance is both inauthentic and alienating; however, there are incentives to do so through management as an ideology. Whereas this could manifest itself in a variety of ways, only one application will be examined in this critique, which is that of being *busy*. Those working in offices appear frequently to be busy, which suggests an organizational bias for employees adopting that behavior. At the most rudimentary level of employment this can be seen in statements like, *if you have time to lean, you have time to clean*. Management as an ideology dictates that workers earn their wages through *productive* labor. There is a correlated aspect of this from the workers' side as well. If one isn't busy, management will quickly assign a new task. To avoid a new task, one might attempt to appear busy. These two distinct motivations combine in a feedback loop in which an individual potentially spends a portion of time simply attempting to appear busy rather than be productive. Performativity, in both *language* and *being*, is consequential to the creation and organizational maintenance of the spectacle of work. Subjugation is essential for its enactment.

As developed in this critique, subjugation exists in two forms in the spectacle of work. The first form is generally well established; therefore, it does not warrant much development. Within organizations, the activities of subordinate workers and managers alike are directed by one's superior(s). This dynamic is stated explicitly within the definition of management, and it is generally expected and accepted. Since this aspect of management is transparent, one can conclude that those who are employed under this form of subjugation made the decision to do so consciously and willfully. The second form of subjugation is obfuscated by management as an ideology and warrants closer examination. While not necessarily explicit in the definition of management, there is an assumption that the direction being given is for the accomplishment of productive work towards a rational objective. Implicit in people's willingness to accept organizational subjugation is the agreement that in so doing, their effort will be directed towards productive aims. As work becomes a spectacle in postmodernity, this assumption becomes increasingly tenuous. Apologists for management as an ideology might say that a subordinate *should* follow the direction of superiors even when the work being directed is apparently irrational or absurd. This defense could be offered on one of several different bases. One might say that a superior has more complete information and that what seems irrational or absurd to a subordinate would become rational or sensible in the context of all available information. There is certainly merit to this position. While it could be argued that sharing the contextual information would be beneficial, it is certainly not a requirement in the general acceptance of management as an ideology. One benefits from taking this point into consideration. Another ground on which one might offer a defense of a subordinate following a seemingly irrational assignment from a superior is more problematic. Under that position, the argument is made that errors are corrected upon identification. If a given superior is making irrational or absurd demands of the subordinate workforce, the issue will become apparent and those at the upper echelons can subsequently correct the managerial *glitch*. This argument is subtler and is often obfuscated in management as an ideology. A healthy degree of confidence in *the system* is required for this defense to have merit. First, one would need to accept the premise that the organization can effectively distinguish between productive work and the appearance of productive work. In short, an organization would need to have the ability to distinguish the *spectacle* from the *real*. Given the complexities of work execution in postmodernity, this is suspect. Second, even if there is a willingness to assume that organizations can effectively make the distinction between accomplishment and artifice, one would then need to have further confidence that the organization would subsequently correct the situation. While apologists for the *status quo* present this situation as if its resolution is self-evident, it isn't really all that clear. This decision, like most business decisions, is the result of a cost-benefit analysis. The ultimate decision rests on which course of action would cause the least amount of focus and damage to management as an ideology. If a superior's directions to subordinates were consistently wide of the mark and consequential, keeping that person in place makes it seem that those at the upper echelons within the organization are inept. If that person is perceived as being misguided or not a good worker, then that person would likely be removed from the position. However, if the superior's directions were inconsistently errant and of little operational consequence, the person might be kept in the position. Why would this be? Implicit in management as an ideology is the assertion that organizational decisions are correct. If those in the upper echelons are required to remove an individual, it is a tacit admission that they made a mistake in putting that person in that position. To some degree, those in the upper echelons would rather subject workers to the manageably irrational incoherence of a superior instead of providing subordinates evidence that management as an ideology is, in fact, an ideology. Once this second form of subjugation is understood, along with its corresponding organizational elements, the alienation of the spectacle of work is increased.

Alienation is a product of the spectacle (Debord, 2005). Organizationally, alienation emerges through the spectacle of work. As discussed previously, it is possible for workers and managers alike to create illusions of productivity. The minimum requirement for the successful illusion is for one to appear busy and to produce something. Management as an ideology creates a structure in which those engaged in the deception might view the situation as being advantageous. Through the process of duplicity, workers get paid for doing *nothing* and that puts them ahead (or winning); however, such a calculation neglects to account for the alienation which is its consequence. Ironically, one can expend as much energy pretending to work as being productive. There is opportunity here for one to become more autonomous. This point is developed more fully in section five, *a path forward*. For now, it is sufficient to acknowledge that the spectacle of work which emerges through management as an ideology contributes to a sense of alienation. While this is not its only consequence, the spectacle of work produces stress that those in the upper echelons will discover that one isn't working. Further, the spectacle of work can contribute to self-doubt as one contemplates one's ability to work versus pretend. This point is developed more fully in section four, *devolving slowly.* Whether it manifests as alienation, stress, or both, the spectacle of work produces negative consequences. Attempts to ignore the nagging effects of the spectacle are persistently haunted by a sense of meaninglessness. Management as an ideology obfuscates the spectacle of work and the corresponding meaninglessness which surrounds it. If left at the subconscious level one becomes trapped by its shadow. Confronting it directly provides a path towards liberation.

Through the spectacle of work, one pretends to be productive which is alienating and reveals that work is *meaningless.* Whereas the short-term effects of such actions are ambiguous, the long-term effects of this could lead to a sense of nihilism. This is developed more fully in section four, *devolving slowly.* For now, it is important to understand that the spectacle of work is linked with a sense of alienation which in turn is linked with a sense of meaninglessness. Such a chain of despair emerges through the enactment of management as an ideology. *Observation* is the linchpin in the spectacle of work. As Foucault (1980) explained, "there is no need for arms, physical violence, material constraints. Just a gaze" (p. 155). The *gaze* enacted through a network of organizational power sets in motion a dynamic of being perpetually busy, producing the spectacle as a consequence. One must appear to be productive at all costs. Under management as an ideology nothing is worse than being *idle.* These dynamics are presented in the détournement, *The Spectacle of Work.*

The Spectacle of Work

Work can feel as if it is executed under a microscope. Organizational power is at its most efficient when its *gaze* has been internalized effectively by all those under its control. The détournement, *The Spectacle of Work*, captures important elements of this phenomenon. The *scientific* background portrays the proclaimed *rigor* and *objectivity* which are foundational legitimations of management as an ideology. From a position outside and above, a manager subjects workers to the persistent gaze of organizational power. Notice how much larger the person in control is as compared to the people working; in fact, the share of space relegated for actual work is the smallest portion of the composition. The relative scale conveys both pay and rhetorical importance. Further, there is a singular individual over the collective in the office denoting that control, under management as an ideology, is embodied in a singular person based on the unique talents of an individual. Conversely, the execution of work is a communal activity in which the people are infinitely replaceable. In *The Spectacle of Work*, the cubicle walls have been removed through the act of organizational surveillance. There is no place to hide from the gazing eye of organizational power. In response, as discussed previously, people's work easily becomes performative – *a spectacle*. The spectacle of work is the process through which one demonstrates to superiors that one is diligent, always busy, but not necessarily productive. It is this work without productivity, which is the essence of *The Spectacle of Work* and is made manifest in (post)modern organizations. Some ways to mitigate it require further exploration.

All work is not the same in terms of its intent and consequence. Some work is strategically aligned and productive, whereas other work is absurd and inconsequential. As previously indicated, the spectacle of work is organizational activity which conveys a sense of being busy but does not contribute meaningfully to organizational performance. Workers and managers alike can engage in the spectacle of work, which emerges from the exercise of organizational power through management as an ideology. The spectacle of work can be made manifest in a variety of ways. Whereas there have always been ways to *slack off* at work, the internet has contributed significantly to the spectacle of work. As Lim, Teo, and Loo (2002) explained, "the availability of the Internet has revolutionized loafing. Specifically, cyberloafing is the IT way of idling on the job, where employees can literally enjoy the best of both worlds by maintaining the guise of being at work while, in effect, traveling through cyberspace for nonwork interests" (p. 67). Sitting at a desk, facing a computer, does not necessarily mean one is *working*. Unless subordinates' computer monitors are visible to the gaze of a superior walking by their cubicle, it is difficult for the superior to know whether a subordinate is actively engaged in work or merely the spectacle of work. It is worth noting that an example of organizational power in action would be the enactment of a policy requiring that employees' cubicles are set up in such a way to facilitate observation of subordinates' computer monitors. Computers and the internet contribute to the spectacle of work in another way. Through the ability to have electronic templates and quick access to data information can be assembled quickly in the form of reports and briefings which are seemingly well researched. Essential to the spectacle of work is the ability to pass off effectively work devoid of real content. In this way, computers function as both a means of distraction and a tool which enables one to compensate for the time consumed being distracted. Whereas the spectacle of work, when effective, will be unnoticed within the organization, not every attempt at achieving the spectacle of work will be successful.

When the spectacle of work is carried out unsuccessfully, the one attempting the ruse could be accused of *loafing*, *slacking*, or *phoning it in*. Consequently, approaches for dealing with these types of organizational behavior potentially provide insight for effectively addressing aspects of the spectacle of work. Since management as an ideology contributes to the spectacle of work, it is perhaps unsurprising to discover that leadership dynamics contribute to addressing this concern. As Lam and Campbell (2021) explained, "how well a leader manages rapport during interactions directly influences whether members in the group are more or less prone to slacking...the relationship between LRM [*leader rapport management*] and social loafing was fully mediated through communication quality" (p. 194). Two elements emerge from the work of Lam and Campbell. First, a lack of *rapport* was found to be associated with greater employee *slacking*. Second, the quality of *communication* was found to be a mediating variable in the relationship. Consistent with this critique of organizational power, rapport and communication can be considered essential elements of *authenticity*. Examining these two elements in more detail will provide insight as to why. Rapport is a close, positive relationship marked by mutual understanding and empathy. When rapport exists, there is a shared affinity among those involved. Establishing and maintaining rapport is facilitated by open and effective communication. Authenticity is central to both rapport and open communication. Part of the development of authenticity is self-reflection. For one to be who one truly is, it is important to understand who that is. Doing so organizationally requires one to step outside the expectations which are implicit in management as an ideology. Assuming self-awareness can be gained through these reflections; a second component is required. Authenticity is not achieved simply by knowing who one *is*. One must *be* authentic. What does this mean in practice? To be authentic in the workplace, one must not only know who one is (achieved through self-reflection), but also *be* one's authentic self at work (achieved through action). Being authentic at work is potentially a risk. It is helpful to think of this as occurring along a spectrum. If one's authentic self is closely aligned with the characteristics an organization desires, there is little risk associated with being authentic. Conversely, if one's authentic self is significantly divergent from those desired attributes, there is substantial risk associated with authenticity. It is beneficial to realize that just as the risk of being authentic occurs along a spectrum, so is authenticity itself. One can be more or less authentic at work. Determining the degree of authenticity one is willing to enact organizationally is likely contingent upon the degree of risk. For the purpose of this critique of organizational power, the focus isn't on the individual determination, but rather on the awareness that as a consequence of management as an ideology one will be confronted with making the choice as part of navigating a career. This is one of the many interpersonal relationships one will encounter which benefits from self-awareness and the ability to regulate responses. As is the case in most human endeavors, the degree to which something is beneficial or detrimental is determinable only within the parameters of a given context. Such is certainly the case as it relates to motivation.

As indicated in section two, *the unbearable banality of management*, motivational posters can produce mockery as well as inspiration. What works for one individual, in one context, might not have the same effect for another individual in a different context. This has implications for the spectacle of work, which is observable in both larger organizations and in smaller teams. Lount and Wilk (2014) noted that, "employee motivation can be both *positively* and *negatively* affected by working in a group. These findings highlight that factors present in the broader organizational context, such as whether or not performance is posted, can in part help to explain when working in a group will *help* or *hurt* employee motivation" (p. 1105, emphasis in original). The work of Lount and Wilk suggests that attempting to combat the spectacle of work through enhanced employee motivation is tricky due to nuances associated with specific organizational contexts. Various elements contribute to the complexity of this task. First, there are inherent differences associated with employees at the individual level. Individual likes, dislikes, sense of humor, education level, area of study, past experiences, organizational status, and future ambitions each potentially contribute to the way in which one responds to organizational attempts at motivation (or coercion). Second, the degree to which organizational culture has been internalized will influence the homogeneity of interpretation and response. Third, the prominence of organizational power will contribute to employee responses to attempted motivation. Fourth, the degree to which management as an ideology is accepted without conscious thought will influence the susceptibility of the workforce to organizational motivation. Lastly, the ability to incorporate *motivation* into one's performance of the spectacle of work will influence its perceived effectiveness. It is worth noting that if one can successfully pretend to work, one can just as easily pretend to be motivated. One could have a meta-performance of the spectacle of work. Collectively, the elements of inherent individual differences, prevalence of organizational culture, power, management as an ideology, and meta-spectacle each contribute to the complexity of effectively using motivation as a means of overcoming the spectacle of work. Another approach, which is developed more fully in section five, *a path forward*, is authenticity and autonomy. For now, it is sufficient to note that these two elements can act as an antidote to the deleterious effects of management as an ideology enacted through organizational power.

The spectacle of work, at the individual task or project level contributes to a sense of *alienation* for those involved in its organizational production. When enacted over an entire career it has cumulative effects which surpass the individual manifestations presented in this critique. These are addressed more fully in section four, *devolving slowly*. Prior to concluding this assessment of the spectacle of work, it is useful to summarize some of its consequences. To do so most effectively, it is beneficial to place these insights in context by returning to its leading theorists. Organizational power enacted through management as an ideology shapes and constrains the channels for career advancement and defines the individual, professional characteristics which are valued. One of the consequences of the spectacle of work is that it produces doubt in the workforce that those who are held in high regard organizationally actually warrant esteem. As Debord (2005) explained, "the admirable people in whom the system personifies itself are well known for not being what they are" (Thesis 61). Part of this insight is ancient in its origin; *one's idols always have feet of clay.* People are flawed; perfection is an unrealistic standard. While disappointing in childhood, most adults learn to admire more generously and are able to accommodate the complexities of those who are respected within a given context. More problematic than this, is the awareness that organizations hold up exemplars not because their illustration is inherently beneficial for those working, but because those that conform to the expectation are beneficial to the organization. To the extent that a gap exists between the perceptions of those working within an organization and the preferences of those at the organization's upper echelons, the spectacle reveals itself for what it is. Management as an ideology attempts to unify what individuals *want* and what the organization *needs.* Stated somewhat differently, management as an ideology attempts to manufacture the exact same wants on the part of its workforce that the organization can provide. As Lyotard (1984) explained, "administrative procedures should make individuals 'want' what the system needs in order to perform well" (p. 62). To the extent to which these *wants* are manufactured by the organization and superimposed on the individual, one becomes increasingly inauthentic as one becomes *successful* organizationally. Once again, management as an ideology obfuscates both this dynamic and its consequence.

III. The Spectacle of Work

Organizational power incentivizes individuals to conform. Management as an ideology seduces people into doing so without conscious thought. The spectacle of work is the nexus of these two dynamics. Through the process a further sense of alienation emerges. This alienation is both *unifying*, as it is pervasive throughout organizations, and *isolating*, as it is seldom discussed openly among those experiencing it. While the particulars of its manifestation will be contingent upon a multitude of factors, its consequence is the same. As Debord (2005) stated:

> What hides under the spectacular oppositions is a *unity of misery*. Behind the masks of total choice, different forms of the same alienation confront each other, all of them built on real contradictions which are repressed. The spectacle exists in a *concentrated* or a *diffuse* form depending on the necessities of the particular stage of misery which it denies and supports. In both cases, the spectacle is nothing more than an image of happy unification surrounded by desolation and fear at the tranquil center of misery. (Thesis 63, emphasis in original)

Misery is a serious concern. Those engaged in human endeavors should pause at its very mention. It is easy for those engaged in business to hide behind objectifications. Concerns for *efficiency*, *profit*, and *optimization* tend to dominate business discussions. Of course, these things matter and warrant attention and consideration. Management as an ideology ensures these elements, and those like them, receive ample organizational attention. But this attention obfuscates as other important concerns are relegated to the margins. For those who are serious about work being ennobling for all those involved in its execution, the aperture of concern must be widened. If management as an ideology incentivizes inauthenticity and the spectacle of work, and if misery is its human consequence, attention needs to be given to this as well. Managers and those being managed are real humans with legitimate needs and concerns.

Actions always produce consequences. The spectacle of work is no different. Can the organization tell the difference between productive work and its spectacle double? Do they care? The consequences of the spectacle of work will be influenced by the answers to these questions. Apart from those organizational consequences, there are personal effects to consider. Like the exhilaration felt when cutting class in high school, there is a certain elation which comes from not getting caught. The first time one doesn't really work at the office, there is a feeling of getting away with it. One might feel like they got paid for doing nothing and view this as a sort of bonus. This might be a *good* feeling once or twice. It doesn't take too many times of *getting away with it*, until one starts to doubt that one's work has any meaning or value. This section examined the alienation which comes from a localized manifestation of the spectacle of work. When the spectacle becomes habitual the consequences are even more concerning. The effects of a prolonged spectacle devolve slowly over the course of one's career.

Key Concepts

- Artifice
- Gaze
- Performativity
- Postmodern
- Spectacle of work
- Rapport

Reflection Questions

1. To what degree have you ever pretended to work when management was around you in the office? What did you do to simulate actual work? Why did you feel compelled to pretend to work when management was around? How did pretending to work make you feel while you were engaged in the simulated work? How did you feel afterwards?
2. Pretending to work could result from a variety of motivations. One could be trying to impress the boss, one could be attempting to avoid additional tasks being assigned, or one might simply be bored, and the act of pretending is a momentary diversion. If you have pretended to work, what was your motivation?
3. In your estimation which does the managerial level above you value more, productivity or the appearance of being productive? To what extent and in what ways does your assessment on this point influence what you do and who you are at work?
4. Think about workers and managers with whom you have a rapport. How does the personal connection of this rapport influence your willingness to engage in the spectacle of

work? Which type of rapport influences your behavior more, that with colleagues or that with your manager? Why do you think that is the case?

5. Does the *spectacle of work* change for professions (e.g., accountant, electrician, engineer, lawyer, mechanic, physician, etc.)? If so, why do you think that those engaged in a profession would have a different response to pretending to work from those engaged in more generalist forms of employment?
6. Effective engagement in another's work likely resides somewhere between micromanagement (i.e., the near constant involvement in every facet of one's work) and *laissez-faire* (i.e., the near absence of any involvement in any facet of one's work). What has been your experience with management along this spectrum? What are your personal inclinations of involvement? How does the spectacle of work vary across the managerial spectrum from micromanagement to *laissez-faire*?

IV. Devolving Slowly

Remembering hope
Life's forward motion promise
Turns its back to all

Transformations, when evolutionary, can be difficult to observe. Nothing in one's life is sufficient preparation for sustaining a career. Examining this numerically is helpful for developing the real context of employment. Depending on when one starts working and when one retires, the length of one's career can easily span a period of 45 to 50 years. Reflecting on common experiences puts this duration into perspective. The number of years devoted to education from K-12 (i.e., compulsory education) is 13 years. If one attended college that might be another 4 to 5 years. In total, one starting a career might have experienced a period of about 18 years in the sustained activity of one's education. Other endeavors likely required substantially less investments of time. So, after one's education, which is likely the single most extensive investment of time in one's life, up until that point, one will start a career which, if everything goes according to plan, will likely last 2.5 times longer in duration than one's previous longest sustained effort. What does this mean? It means that a person starting a career really has no lived experience from which to understand just how long this portion of one's life will last, or just how long it will feel. If one takes a lifetime of 90 years and breaks it into thirds (i.e., the ages 0-30, 31-60, 61-90), one starts one's career in *youth* and concludes it in *old age*. Whereas people will execute a career with varying levels of investment, for some it will be the most important thing, for others it will be less so, for most a career is a significant part of one's *lifetime*. As the ancient Ionian philosopher Heraclitus observed, *no person ever steps in the same river twice*. In much the same way, the person entering an organization for a career will not be the same individual who leaves, even if the two share the same name, fingerprints, and social security number. Nobody can escape the transformations, organic and organizational, which occur through sustained exposure to organizational power as enacted through management as an ideology. There is opportunity for work to be ennobling. When this occurs, one retires *better* than one arrived. When the spectacle of work is enacted over the course of one's career, one *devolves slowly* into a version which is, in some ways, *less than* when one started. Understanding this concern is an important step in being able to effectively address it individually and organizationally.

Whereas aspects of work are the primary focus in this section, it is essential to acknowledge that longevity itself can be its own source of deterioration. Eyesight, hearing, physical strength, as well as mental and other physical capabilities decline with time after a certain point. Management as an ideology acknowledges some attributes associated with declining work performance as a function of time. Research related to this topic has addressed, among other things, the interrelated issues of stress (Barnes-Farrell, Rumery & Swody, 2002; Hauk, Göritz & Krumm, 2019; Robson & Hansson, 2007; Schmitz, McCluney, Sonnega & Hicken, 2019), poor work-life balance (Figueredo, García-Ael, Gragnano & Topa, 2021; Hovbrandt, Håkansson, Albin, Carlsson & Nilsson, 2019; Schilling, 2015), health ailments and risks (Berthung, Gutacker, Friborg, Abelsen & Olsen, 2021; Lohela-Karlsson, Nybergh & Jensen, 2018; Nilsen et al., 2014; Sharma, Kaur, Kaur & Kaur, 2014), and reduced productivity (Honda et al., 2021; Ranasinghe et al., 2016; Xiang et al., 2020). Those starting, or midway through, their careers benefit from reflecting upon these concerns. Whereas one can do things which influence the likelihood and consequence of these issues, in some respects these elements are unavoidable. Aging and the corresponding loss of some acuity are expected. In fact, it is this aspect of these concerns which make it most interesting as a point of reflection. It is not likely coincidental that it is exactly those things which are largely inherent and inevitable that management as an ideology is willing to acknowledge. Further, since there is a biological component to these concerns, organizational power can direct the focus on the individual and away from the organization. These issues are clearly important, but they are radically different from the deleterious effects which devolve slowly through prolonged enactment of the spectacle of work. It is precisely because management as an ideology is willing to acknowledge the issues of stress, work-life balance, individual health concerns, and reduced productivity that those interested in a critique of organizational power benefit from turning their gaze elsewhere. Power directs attention to those areas which are easiest to defend. Pretending to work can create its own stressors, fatigue, and psychological implications. Prolonged engagement with the spectacle of work is obfuscated by management as an ideology and therefore warrants closer scrutiny.

As indicated in section three, *the spectacle of work*, one can experience alienation at the individual task or project level, but when one enacts the spectacle over the course of an entire career it has cumulative effects which surpass those experienced immediately. The two major consequences of a prolonged execution of the spectacle presented here are an erosion of confidence in one's abilities and a sense of meaninglessness associated with one's work. Time becomes an important variable in this context. Proficiency is achieved with time. Through confronting organizational challenges, one's skills are developed and refined. Over the course of a career, one might even develop *expertise*. The spectacle of work precludes the development of one's craft, as one instead gains proficiency in subterfuge. At first, there is a tremendous gap between what one *can do* and what one accomplishes through the spectacle of work. Project after project, this distance shrinks until one is uncertain that one can do anything other than pretend to work. One becomes entrapped in the spectacle of work through the atrophy of their capabilities and confidence. Once this stage is reached, the spectacle of work is perpetuated more by its own inertia than by willful, personal action. Organizational habits are hard to break. As this situation repeats itself and devolves with time a sense of meaninglessness associated with one's work can emerge. If work is to be ennobling its execution must serve some purpose; the individual must understand the purpose and feel that one's efforts contribute to the positive outcome. The contribution does not need to be large. Making even a small contribution to a worthy endeavor is sufficient for a sense of pride. The spectacle of work precludes this. It is a small step for one to make from being engaged in meaningless work to feeling that oneself is meaningless. As indicated in section three, *the spectacle of work*, one never gets away with anything even if one is never caught by those in positions of authority. One always knows one's *truth*. It is challenging to feel that one is doing something meaningful with one's finite existence if the preponderance of one's labor and life are consumed executing meaningless tasks. As Camus (1991) explained, "there is no more dreadful punishment than futile and hopeless labor" (p. 119). When this is realized, there are a couple of responses available. One could attempt to regain meaning in one's employment or seek fulfillment outside of work as one effectively gives up on establishing a sense of professional accomplishment. If this occurs, organizational nihilism is likely close behind.

Sustained confrontation with meaninglessness in one's daily work potentially devolves slowly into organizational nihilism. But what is nihilism, and to what extent (*if any*) does it relate to management as an ideology and organizational power? Definitions of nihilism vary based on context and intent. Given the close connection between nihilism and the philosophy of Nietzsche, it is constructive to start our understanding with his conceptualization. *Nihilism*, for Nietzsche (1968), is "the radical repudiation of value, meaning, and desirability" (p. 7), in which "the highest values devalue themselves" (p. 9). Two terms are essential here: *radical* and *repudiation*. While common usages of the term radical tend to focus on an extreme position (e.g., a political radical), historically the term has focused on aspects related to, or proceeding from, the *root*. This notion of radical takes aim at the *essence* of its target of inquiry. Within this context, repudiation can be understood as a rejection or denial. From this perspective, Nietzsche's construction of nihilism focuses attention on a rejection of the core of a given value structure. This holds consequential implications for management as an ideology, as "every fruitful and powerful movement of humanity has also created at the same time a nihilistic movement" (Nietzsche, p. 69). Given the pervasiveness of management as an ideology, it is expected that its use through organizational power would engender a nihilistic response. In an examination of linkages between Nietzsche's constructions of power and international business ethics, Jackson and Reboulet (2019) defined nihilism as "a philosophical commitment in which one rejects the notion of *inherent* meaning" (p. 31, emphasis in original). The elements of *philosophical commitment* and *inherent meaning* are worthy of additional focus. First, as noted by Jackson and Reboulet, nihilism is an intellectual position staked by an individual. Second, its focus is on a lack of inherent meaning. What does this mean? Nihilism is often described as the position that things are meaningless. Jackson and Reboulet's focus on *inherent* meaning creates space for one to create meaning, which is the focus of existentialist philosophy, while acknowledging that things, *in-and-of-themselves*, have no meaning. As discussed in section three, the essence of the spectacle of work is that one engages in pretense. This could be enacted transparently, while operating entirely unacknowledged, through management as an ideology. Baudrillard's (1994) construction is useful for examining aspects of organizationally operationalized nihilism. As Baudrillard explained:

> Today's nihilism is one of transparency, and it is in some sense more radical, more crucial than in its prior and historical forms, because this transparency, this irresolution is indissolubly that of the system, and that of all the theory that still pretends to analyze it...nihilism has been entirely realized no longer through destruction, but through simulation and deterrence. (p. 159)

Transparency and *simulation* are central to Baudrillard's construction of nihilism. These notions are captured well by the following apocryphal story. President Nixon was giving a speech at a hotel conference room in the early 1970s. A youthful crowd protesting the Vietnam War was becoming riotous. Secret Service agents were being overrun. President Nixon escaped by ducking through the hotel kitchen wearing a rubberized *Nixon Mask*. This story illustrates a simulated doubling which is the essence of the *transparency* of nihilism residing at the core of the spectacle of work which devolves slowly over the course of a career.

There is a common insight that, *the best place to hide something is in plain sight*. Sustaining the spectacle of work is facilitated by the simulated transparency, discussed by Baudrillard, in which one *hides* in plain sight. If an employee is flagrantly unproductive, that employee would likely be removed. As discussed, management as an ideology requires that one always appears to be busy. As discussed previously in section three, *the spectacle of work*, one can appear to be busy while accomplishing nothing. There is another way in which this could unfold, which is more complex. One could be flagrantly unproductive, and even project an aura of being flagrantly unproductive within an organization, if one's superiors interpret the appearance of unproductivity as masking *real* productivity. Essential to this dynamic is that the organization is unable to effectively distinguish between *real* and *simulated* work, and that the spectacle of work is organizationally secure. What is somewhat paradoxical is that such an individual may be promoted quickly within the organization. This person might exude a sense of *confidence*, *charm*, *strength*, or *mysteriousness*, which management as an ideology values. Since this individual is unencumbered by the execution of actual work, one has ample time to cultivate one's organizational *persona* or *brand*. What is useful for *winning* the *game* of organizational advancement, is not necessarily aligned well with what is fulfilling. As one focuses increasing attention on what it takes to *get ahead* organizationally, less attention (by definition) will be available to expend on determining who one is and what one honestly wants from a career and life. This is not accidental. Management as an ideology wants to distract workers first by enticing them with ever increasingly large *carrots*, and if that doesn't work, by threatening them with more painful *sticks*. Through this dressage organizational power shapes and constrains the focus of individuals towards the *game* of advancement in which the spectacle of work is enacted over the course of one's career. The devolution of which is beneficial to understand in terms of its immediate and long-term consequences.

Devolution can be understood broadly as a process of degeneration, culminating in a worse situation. Organizationally, devolution could be associated with a reduction in quality or performance, while individually, it could be associated with despair or nihilism. Management as an ideology obfuscates the devolution of the spectacle of work by focusing attention on organizational progress and personal advancement. If one measures enough things, it is never difficult to be able to point to one metric which happens to be improving. Despite the rhetoric of improvement in management as an ideology what is enacted and experienced individually through the spectacle of work could be characterized as retrograde. It should be stated explicitly that the concept of devolution betrays a preference. In a value-free sense, one could simply discuss organizational change. That things are different does not necessitate that they are *better* or *worse*. The relative valuation is intentional here. In using the term *devolution*, a negative connotation is invoked purposively. The perpetuation of the spectacle of work over the course of a career reflects subjugation and produces alienation. This engenders nihilism as one moves further away from authenticity and autonomy. Organizational power attempts to distract participants in the system through management as an ideology. Placing management in quandary reveals traces of this dynamic. When workers and managers sustain the spectacle of work longer than they are psychologically able, a sense of occupational burnout results. The concern of burnout will be addressed after the presentation of the détournement, *Devolving Slowly*, which places the concept of devolution in its biological sense as a metaphor for this existential decline.

Devolving Slowly

Sustaining work as a spectacle over a prolonged period leaves a mark. In fact, it is transformative. The détournement, *Devolving Slowly*, conveys this metaphorically as a degression from human to ape. Within this office setting, all the trappings of work have been removed. There are no cubicles, computers, phones, or *motivational* posters. All that remains is a void of organizational space with a slowly devolving human. Entering the office upright, one is excited about the future, and confident in one's abilities. After 45 years of drudgery associated with perpetually enacting the spectacle of work, one exits hunched, dull, and *simian*. All the latent potential for the development of skill and expertise through an ennobling profession has been squandered. While management as an ideology, through the channels of organizational power, focuses collective attention upon prioritizing responses to exigencies and planning long-term strategic visions, little attention is given to the human consequences to those engaged in work over the course of a career. Organizationally, the most pressing consequence is burnout.

Burnout can occur at any time or level within an organization. Nobody is immune from its occurrence or consequence. This is a concern with organizational and existential dimensions. Burnout is an organizational concern insofar as its occurrence affects productivity negatively. Existentially, burnout is distressing as it diminishes one's quality of life. Taken together, these two facets suggest that focusing attention on understanding and reducing organizational burnout is a legitimate organizational concern. This exploration of burnout is focused upon how the prolonged enactment of the spectacle of work contributes to the development of burnout. Management as an ideology obfuscates burnout; a critique of organizational power reveals it for what it is, a natural consequence of the spectacle of work. To understand burnout more fully, it is useful to first define it operationally. Following its linguistic delimitation, an articulation of how it emerges and where it resides in the organizational hierarchy is provided. Once it is defined and situated, a strategy for addressing it is presented. Central to this aspect of burnout is an appreciation as to how authenticity and autonomy help to mitigate its emergence and effect.

As discussed in section three, *the spectacle of work*, workers and lower-echelon managers are both subjugated by those at higher echelons within organizations. Research provides corroborating evidence for this perspective, as burnout is negatively correlated with organizational position. Collectively, these insights provide a starting point for examining burnout. Turning first to its definition provides the most efficient inroad for understanding.

There is a reductionist tendency to shrink complexity as much as possible. At an extreme, multifaceted concerns are condensed to a single element. Often important nuance is sacrificed in the process. While the element singled out for focus is likely part, perhaps the majority even, of the phenomenon of inquiry, subtlety is lacking. The neglected elements are lost in the process which limits understanding and potential areas of improvement. In dealing with burnout, it is important to avoid this error in conceptualization. Organizational burnout is not monolithic. As Matthews, Beeler, Zablah, and Hair (2018) explained, "burnout is composed of three related dimensions: emotional exhaustion, depersonalization, and personal accomplishment" (p. 304). Each element reveals a vital aspect of burnout. First, burnout emerges through a process of emotional exhaustion. Initially people are personally invested in the organization and become worn down over time. Understanding that organizations consume as much as one is willing to give is beneficial. An organization's appetite for people's effort is insatiable. It will always consume more. If an individual does not monitor this for oneself, emotional exhaustion can ensue. A second component of burnout is depersonalization. This is observable in the spectacle of work. If one is engaged in work which lacks meaning it stands to reason that one would want to distance oneself from its creation. In some respects, depersonalization can be understood as intentional alienation. In the case of depersonalization, a person no longer wants to be associated with the product of one's labor. Whether this emerges through embarrassment or fatigue, the act of emotionally distancing oneself from the work which under management as an ideology is supposed to be both financially rewarding and personally fulfilling, is certainly a warning sign. Lastly, a diminished sense of personal accomplishment contributes to burnout. It is a small step from this dwindling of pride in one's work to the nihilism presented previously. Collectively, these three elements provide enhanced granularity for understanding organizational burnout. Building on this understanding of the component elements of burnout, it is beneficial to examine how it emerges.

As previously described, a career unfolds over a period the length of which those at the beginning have no context for understanding. Management as an ideology aims to lock employees into a course of unquestioning compliance. Whereas the dressage of organizational power compels them to always be busy, the spectacle of work allows for this effort to be an illusion and the effort to be of no productive organizational effect. Enacting the spectacle over the course of one's career results in a slow devolution. Its corrosive effects do not appear instantaneously. Nor do they appear uniformly. For many engaged in a prolonged performance of the spectacle of work burnout will eventually ensue. If it does, burnout could be experienced as a compounding effect, which is easy to deal with at first but subsequently overwhelming. As Cordes, Dougherty, and Blum (1997) explained, "burnout is a developmental process. There is no on-off switch, no clearly defined moment at which an employee announces 'I am *burned* out'. It is, rather, a gradual eroding process" (p. 699, emphasis in original). In this gradual eroding process, one will have good days and bad days at work, days which are closer to the excitement and joy one had at the beginning of one's career, and days in which one feels hopeless about its trajectory and content. Management as an ideology obfuscates this, attempting to convince those experiencing burnout that, *everybody has bad days*. Burnout is different. Of course, those engaged in any activity will have bad days. Things don't always go right, and frustrations can distract one from appreciating how fortunate one is. Burnout is not ingratitude; it is the mental and physical awareness that one can no longer existentially sustain the *status quo*. Whereas it would be imprudent to quit at the first sign of annoyance, it is intolerable to waste one's finite existence toiling in vain and accomplishing nothing meaningful. There are no easy answers here. If one has a *bad* day at work, one benefits from not overanalyzing it. If one starts to experience more bad days than good, and looks ahead and experiences a sense of dread rather than excitement, this is likely an indication that something is amiss. For one to make this determination accurately, it is useful to parse a distinction about burnout.

Management as an ideology obfuscates burnout. When elements of burnout become too pronounced to ignore, organizational power directs focus towards the individual to *gaslight* its victim. The focus of the *problem* is on the individual performing the work and not on the content of the work itself or the way in which the work is enacted organizationally. Organizations might acknowledge that an individual is burned out, but frame this as being a consequence of the assigned work being too much or too difficult *for* the individual. There is something of value worth exploring here. Management as an ideology protects the privilege and legitimacy of organizational power through its ability to define situations. By focusing on the *for the individual* aspect of burnout management as an ideology effectively obfuscates the *assigned work* portion of the phenomenon. This is classic victim blaming. The workload was, after all, assigned by the organization through the managerial process. Additionally, having a significant amount of challenging work isn't inherently a source of burnout, as it could also contribute to the most rewarding and energizing of career accomplishments. Burnout is not simply a function of the quantity and difficulty of the assigned tasks, but also its inherent quality. As Skok, Zoroja, and Bach (2013) described, "burnout effect affects individuals when they work hard and become exhausted, frustrated and unproductive. It is not just a problem of a lot of work but the attitude the person has towards its work and obligations" (p. 278). By focusing on the components of burnout which can be attributed to an individual, management as an ideology obfuscates that at least some of the work is inherently ungratifying. Of course, some necessary work is potentially unglamourous and unfulfilling. People often execute this type of work with stoic reserve and dignity. The issue isn't really with that aspect of work, but rather with the way management as an ideology obfuscates this organizationally. Burnout emerges in the gap between the organizational rhetoric and reality associated with assigned tasks. When the organization, through management as an ideology, claims that all work is important, but individuals observe that it clearly isn't, it is reasonable that one would become burned out. There are numerous examples of how this unfolds daily. Reports that took months to research and produce collect dust on a shelf. Efforts to improve performance are abandoned after the planning phase. A red-hot tasker which required one to work through the weekend is completely ignored on Monday when the higher-echelon manager becomes distracted by something else. All share a common element. Management as an ideology using organizational power directs individuals to produce products which are subsequently ignored. Over the course of a career this makes it challenging, if not absurd, for one to be personally invested. While this response is understandable it is not beneficial organizationally or personally. This is addressed in section five, *a path forward*. For now, it is sufficient to note that the dynamic which produces burnout is inherent in management as an ideology which directs individuals to do whatever they are told but places no constraint on those at the upper echelon of organizations to use or even acknowledge it. Once again, it is not simply the workers who experience this, but managers at lower echelons as well. For managers the situation is doubled as they experience it from those above and below them within an organization, increasing the likelihood of burnout.

One of the central focal points of this critique is how management as an ideology seduces people into the managerial ranks, and that upon entering lower-echelon, management positions one is confronted with a situation which is in some respects little different from the subordinate positions, and in some ways worse. Regarding burnout, this dynamic is complex and not altogether consistent. Korman, Van Quaquebeke, and Troester (2021) noted that "managers are less affected by burnout than non-managers, and...managers at the top are even less endangered" (p. 16). Their research suggests that burnout generally maps to the organizational hierarchy, with more pronounced burnout being experienced at the lower positions and incrementally less burnout experienced in positions at the upper echelons of an organization. This suggests that as one can have greater autonomy one can protect oneself from burnout. This point is developed more fully subsequently. Whereas this insight is promising for management as an ideology, there are still concerns which warrant examination. As Pelletier-Bosshard, Freeman, Jauvin, and Côté, (2021) explained, those in management experience "helplessness, as well as a certain habituation to the constrained context, which could lead to some reluctance to endeavor to change the situation," and that "middle managers have to find a way of juggling their accountability to senior managers with their representation of staff" (p. 156). There are elements upon which to focus here. Central to the predicament of middle managers is a sense of *helplessness*. This calls into the question the assumed agency afforded to management in terms of task autonomy. Second, middle managers are perpetually *juggling* the tensions which exist between those above them and those below them within an organization. A sustained balancing of the competing demands between these two disparate groups is challenging. The task is compounded in complexity and consequence if one is doing so within the spectacle of work. Interestingly, when confronting these challenges managers might eschew the very resources one routinely suggests to one's subordinates.

Advice is notoriously easy to give and hard to follow. Part of this dynamic is straightforward enough as it reflects little more than a relatively benign aspect of human cognition. Insight is a function of position and stress. When one is outside a given predicament, one can see better the issue, its context, and what resources are available both to help in its resolution and to aid the individual as the issue is resolved. Enmeshed directly in that same predicament, one is too overwhelmed to think clearly. Whereas there is little to critique with this aspect of advice, there is a darker, organizational aspect which warrants increased scrutiny. In the following example, giving all those involved the benefit of the doubt, let's assume that sincere advice is being given that would, in fact, be of benefit to the person receiving the advice. When a superior provides advice to a subordinate, the superior has a degree of confidence that the given advice will not be detrimental to the subordinate. The basis of this determination resides in a self-assessment. To the degree that the eventual consequences would be created and administered through the superior, this confidence is likely appropriate. This same individual, when receiving advice as a subordinate from one's superior, does not have the same confidence. The basis of this determination resides in an assessment of *the system*. Such a situation can create cognitive dissonance as a lower-echelon manager expects subordinates to trust in the system the manager doubts. Management as an ideology obfuscates that the same phrase, *trust me, the system is here to help you*, is viewed as legitimate by lower-echelon managers when they say it to their subordinates, but rings hollow when they hear it from their superiors. As Pelletier-Bosshard, Freeman, Jauvin, and Côté (2021) explained, "It seems paradoxical that managers themselves do not necessarily seek or have access to the type of support that they advocate for their staff" (p. 158). The rhetoric required by management may be incongruent. The spectacle of work, enacted over the course of career, can lead to nihilism and burnout. This occurs for workers and managers alike. This situation can be further complicated for managers as there is the potential for cognitive dissonance and a sense of hypocrisy when one counsels subordinates to do something which one is unwilling to do oneself. While this concern is serious and consequential, there is some hope for dealing with it more constructively within organizations.

Whereas burnout can occur anywhere within an organization, its occurrence is neither equally likely nor random. This has consequences for workers and lower-echelon managers within organizations. As reported previously, research by Korman, Van Quaquebeke, and Troester (2021) suggests that the experience of burnout is less pronounced as one ascends the organizational hierarchy. This means that the higher up one is in the organization, the less likely it is that one will experience organizational burnout. There are structural aspects which likely contribute to this phenomenon. Two of these elements will be examined briefly prior to exploring one of the key themes of this critique of organizational power. First, perspective and context are enhanced at higher echelons within organizations as information is aggregated and synthesized. This provides those holding higher-echelon positions with a more robust vantage point from which to understand how one's work contributes to organizational outcomes, which in turn reduces the occurrence of burnout. Second, higher-echelon positions are more wide-ranging which enables greater variety in terms of executed tasks and focus. Being able to switch among a variety of concerns enables those in higher-echelon positions to mitigate burnout more effectively. This second point provides a useful transition point as it is both structural, insofar as the position itself is multifaceted, but also reflects how autonomy provides an antidote against organizational burnout. As indicated, being able to transition among a variety of activities enables one to break up the monotony of any given task. For those in higher-echelon positions, the switching among tasks is seldom directed, but rather is freely enacted at one's discretion. In short, the individual has the autonomy needed to prevent the occurrence of burnout. Matthews, Beeler, Zablah, and Hair (2018) explained, autonomy reduces burnout as, "it gives employees control over their daily work life" (p. 304). One of the central critiques of organizational power enacted through management as an ideology is that it effectively precludes individuals from the autonomy which enhances professional fulfillment. The work of Matthews, Beeler, Zablah, and Hair highlights that autonomy holds the potential to reduce organizational burnout. This in turn can improve both organizational performance and existential well-being. Tension arises because autonomy strikes at the core of management as an ideology. If people can handle the freedom to execute organizational work of their choosing, along their selected project timeline, what is the need or value of management? Autonomy places *management in quandary*. Addressing this quandary requires at least one last examination of the power which permeates existing organizational structures.

The long-term effects presented here, which devolve slowly through the persistent enactment of the spectacle of work, occur in bureaucracies and corporations alike. In terms of structure, a false dichotomy is perpetuated between government bureaucracies on one side and corporate organizations on the other. Because there is a categorical difference in terms of their respective teleologies, the assumption is generally made that structural differences emerge consequently. Whereas bureaucracies are driven by mission and corporations by profit, in terms of organizational power and management as an ideology there is little (maybe no) appreciable difference between the two types of organizations. The organizational structure, held in common between bureaucracies and corporations, is the one which enhances organizational power and facilitates the widest and most efficient dissemination of management as an ideology. In this important respect, there is no difference between the two. As Hummel (2008) explained, "we spend most of our working day in bureaucracies: modern organizations whether public or private, governmental or corporate or non-profit. There we are unmade and transformed" (p. xx). In addition to the structural similarities already examined, Hummel's insight is useful insofar as it brings focus to the way in which individuals are *transformed* within organizations. As stated at the beginning of this section, these transformations are difficult to observe on a day-to-day basis and can be quite jarring when presented as a beginning-end comparison. If one wants to effectively confront these concerns, an accurate assessment of the situation is required. Management as an ideology obfuscates much of the structure and consequence of organizational power.

This critique has pointed out key pressure points within *the system*. Perhaps one of the greatest hurdles to overcome is the simple, shared desire to believe that things are different from how they are. Hummel noted that, "a delusion is that, whatever the faults of modern organizations, these are just anomalies that can be fixed. We all subscribe to this delusion. Without it there is no hope." (p. 3). There are systematic issues which are produced through the enactment of management as an ideology. These occur in both bureaucracies and corporations. Overcoming them requires at least two things. First, those experiencing the negative effects of organizational power need to be able to operate outside management as an ideology to identify what they are experiencing and then have the courage to acknowledge it. Second, these individuals need to address it effectively. Addressing these concerns effectively has individual, collective, and organizational components. Some thoughts on this are presented in the following section, *a path forward*. For now, it is sufficient to note that how organizations experience these concerns, and ultimately what organizations value, is categorically different from the individuals who inhabit and socially enact the organization. Braverman (1974) captured *when* and *why* issues become organizational concerns by noting, "for corporate management this is a problem in costs and controls, not in the 'humanization of work.' It compels their attention because it manifests itself in absentee, turnover, and productivity levels" (p. 36). For *existential concerns* to become *organizational problems*, one must translate them into the language of organizational power. Otherwise, management as an ideology will categorize these legitimate concerns as nothing more than another voice in an endless stream of complaints one is able to ignore with prejudice.

As introduced in section three, *the spectacle of work*, and extended here in section four, *devolving slowly*, being observed transforms the way work is enacted. Observation is essential to the managerial tasks of organizing and controlling, and it is accepted unquestioningly by those adhering to management as an ideology. Embodying managerial functions in a single individual is useful administratively as it provides a solitary reference point. This has organizational value, as does having a workforce vying for those coveted positions. This critique of organizational power has illustrated that subjugation and alienation are created and sustained through management as an ideology. Likewise, throughout this critique the notions of authenticity and autonomy emerge as humanist virtues which not only hold the potential to improve existential well-being but also improve organizational performance. Without those important elements, the spectacle of work tends to devolve slowly into nihilism and burnout. In confronting these concerns, time is a variable with which one must contend. Time is relative. A duration is *long* or *short* only in comparison to something else. Even if a person's career spans 45 to 50 years, one is still only a *temporary* worker, in the sense that one's employment will eventually come to an end. Organizations persist indefinitely. Structures maintain and perpetuate ideologies. There is an asymmetry in the time horizon between an organization and those who inhabit and enact it. Organizational power emerges, in part, through its potentially infinite persistence which is beholden to no specific individual or collective for its perpetuation. Management as an ideology contributes to this continuity. A critique of organizational power reveals management as an ideology. Confronting management as an ideology provides alternatives which hold the potential to enhance authenticity and autonomy. These twin virtues hold the key for existential well-being and organizational performance and are antidotes to the spectacle of work and its deleterious effects which devolve slowly over the course of careers. This is presented more fully in section five, *a path forward*. Prior to presenting that path forward, it is useful to summarize some of the key insights developed through the slow devolution of the spectacle of work.

One never leaves an organization as the same person one was upon entering. Daily these changes are nearly impossible to detect. Over the course of a career, they can hardly be ignored. Perhaps older, wiser, and richer, or maybe broken, cynical, and despairing, in a multitude of ways work is transformative. For better or worse the dressage of organizational power alters the individuals who work there. Management as an ideology entices people to pursue managerial positions, engage in the spectacle of work, and devolve slowly into nihilism and burnout. In its current state, management as an ideology leaves too many working individuals wanting for something better. It doesn't have to be this way. One can regain a sense of agency and improve the situation for oneself and others. If work is to be ennobling, there must be increased space for authenticity and autonomy. To confront this challenge effectively one must understand the nature of organizational power. Overcoming the negative effects of management as an ideology will not come from the acquiescence of those in authority. Freedom is never given. The very process of *asking* only entrenches further the organizational dynamics of power one is attempting to overcome. To ask is to subordinate and constrain. Authenticity and autonomy are not benefits those in power grant, rather, they are virtues one lives. These virtues, while nonnegotiable, are not limitless. One's authenticity and autonomy, if they are to be sustainable organizationally, need to harmonize with those of others, and contribute to organizational performance. Within these parameters however, there is ample room to improve how work is enacted organizationally. Doing so requires *a path forward*.

Key Concepts

- Bureaucracy
- Burnout
- Corporations
- Devolution
- Expertise
- Nihilism
- Reductionist
- Subterfuge

Reflection Questions

1. What is the longest amount of time you were engaged in the pursuit of a single goal (e.g., Eagle Scout, The Gold Award, basic training, college, professional certification, etc.)? At any point did you feel like giving up? What was your motivation?
2. Basic training lasts ~12 weeks, college ~4-5 years, and achieving the highest ranks in scouting can take up to 12 years. Each of these requires a sustained investment of time. Now think of a 45-year career. None of the listed efforts come close to that amount of time. How will you sustain interest in your career over such an extended period?
3. Think of a time when you were bored. How did you respond? Would your actions be described as productive or destructive? What would you do differently if you could?
4. Compare and contrast your conceptualizations of bureaucracies and corporations. In this section, it is asserted that, in terms of organizational power and management as an ideology

there is little difference between the two and that the organizational structure, held in common is the one which enhances organizational power and facilitates the widest and most efficient dissemination of management as an ideology. Do you agree with this statement? Why or why not?

5. When one has retired on the job, there is the potential for an extended performance in which the employee pretends to work, and the manager pretends not to notice that the person isn't working. What are some of the personal and organizational consequences associated with this dynamic?
6. If you could "get away with it," and not produce anything of value at work, would you? What do you think the long-term consequence to one's self-assessment would be of knowing that one was employed for ten, twenty, or thirty years without really making a meaningful contribution? In the end, is it possible to "get away" with anything?

V. A Path Forward

Obstruct not your eyes
Each journey requires resolve
To care with passion

Alternatives to the *status quo* exist. Management as an ideology, while dominant, is not the only way of thinking and being. Organizational power can be confronted directly and indirectly. In fact, people in organizations overcome the deleterious effects of management as an ideology daily in a multitude of ways. What is presented here in section five, is *a* path forward. It should be noted that it isn't offered as *the* path forward. Organizational reality is too complex and varied for a single solution to work universally. The purpose of this section is not to provide a guidebook for tactical action, but rather a critique to inform strategic thinking from which personal and collective action will more effectively emerge. Prior to presenting that information, it is useful to review the key elements presented thus far in this sustained critique of organizational power as it is operationalized through management as an ideology. Section one, *squares in cubes*, focused on management from a subordinate's perspective, whereas section two, *the unbearable banality of management*, focused on management from a manager's perspective. These two sections highlighted the subjugation, alienation, and power dynamics inherent between superiors and subordinates. Section three, *the spectacle of work*, brought attention to the performative aspects of employment, and section four, *devolving slowly*, highlighted the entropic nature of sustaining that spectacle over the duration of one's career, which likely culminates with nihilism and burnout. Collectively, these four sections highlighted challenges associated with the way modern management is enacted. At each turn, authenticity and autonomy were found to be antidotes to the subjugation and alienation which emerge from management as an ideology. To understand the path forward presented here, it is useful to first review some of the suggestions which are offered through traditional management research. Following that review, this concern is situated both in its broader humanistic perspective and in its structural context. From that review it is possible to address proposed changes to organizations as starting as utopian and culminating as dystopian. Lastly, *a path forward* is presented.

Attempts to improve management are not new. In an organizational sense, it is useful to assess from where the efforts were made and for what purpose. In terms of the location from which are attempts to improve management are made one can generalize this as from either *inside* or *outside* the system. Why does this matter? In short, systems frequently ignore *suggestions* which come from outside its domain. Whereas there are plenty of reasons to rail against this tendency (e.g., elitist, exclusionary), there is one simple reason organizations tend to adopt this stance towards external critiques. Since those from outside the system have not experienced the situation(s) directly, their perspectives are easy to marginalize institutionally as being naïve or academic; however, there is a complicating factor to this. The critiques from those within a given organization are marginalized too, but this time based on it simply being characterized as disgruntled complaining. So, for a critique to have a viable chance of being considered seriously, it must come from within the system (i.e., from somebody with direct experience), but outside the organization (i.e., somebody objective). This is a rather narrow corridor, and it helps explain why management as an ideology has remained largely unchanged. As for the purpose, organizations tend to prefer incremental changes *within* the system to radical changes *of* the system. In other words, critiques of the system are viewed as attacks, to which institutions mobilize defensive responses. A change within the system is typically viewed as an opportunity for improvement. Consequently, in terms of both the location from where a critique comes and its directed purpose, organizations exhibit an inherent conservatism, in the sense that effort is made to maintain the *status quo*. From perspectives largely within the system, research related to improving management theory and praxis has focused on aspects including fostering team ownership (Brennan & Wendt, 2021; Curcuruto & Griffin, 2018; Paul, Niehoff & Turnley, 2000), improving delegation (Eiser, 2008; Kane-Urrabazo, 2006; Um-e-Rubbab & Naqvi, 2020; Yoon, Kim & Shin, 2016), embracing mistakes (Collins, Block, Arnold & Christakis, 2009; Munro, 2019; Scalliet, 2006), and enhancing employee motivation (Buzády & Georgiu, 2011; Graves & Luciano, 2013; Sawhney & Michel, 2021; Sihag, 2016). Such attempts at improvement are institutionally acceptable insofar as they perpetuate organizational power through management as an ideology. Forming a viable path forward for improving the situation for workers and lower-echelon managers requires an accurate assessment of where one is, and what is reasonably possible. Such an assessment is never easy. As Alinsky (1989) explained, "it is painful to accept fully the simple fact that one begins from where one is, that one must break free of the web of illusions one spins about life" (p. 12). Sections one through four were designed to help one *break free* from the illusions one has about work, management, and power. To prepare for the suggestions developed subsequently in this section, it is useful to extend this critique to address some macrolevel concerns related to economic and existential dynamics which contribute to the perpetuation of management as an ideology.

As indicated previously, organizations are conservative in the sense that there are internal dynamics which function to maintain the *status quo*. This inherent stabilizing effect perpetuates management as an ideology through organizational power. Whereas this critique has focused on the manifestation of this phenomenon in an organizational sense, it is beneficial in terms of subsequent action to understand any specific organizational occurrence is a microlevel incident which occurs within a broader macrolevel context. The dynamics occurring within organizations are a cause and consequence of the consumer economy in which employees *work* to *buy* in a perpetual cycle of expenditures and debt requiring continued employment and income. As Marcuse (1969) described, "the so-called consumer economy and the politics of corporate capitalism have created a second nature of man which ties him libidinally and aggressively to the commodity form," with the insight that "the needs generated by this system are thus eminently stabilizing, conservative needs...the market has always been one of exploitation and thereby of domination, insuring the class structure of society" (p. 11). The insight explained by Marcuse reveals what management as an ideology obfuscates, namely, that whereas a few might advance to the upper echelons through employment, most will simply work in a form which perpetuates the *class structure of society*. Hierarchies are increasingly narrow at the top. It is a mathematical fact that most people at the bottom will not advance. Management as an ideology incentivizes competition among one's peers as a means of acquiring one of the few coveted positions at the top rather than encouraging solidarity which holds the potential to benefit all those at lower organizational strata. Whereas the consumer economy creates a structural reason for subjugation, it is important to appreciate that individuals play a role as well. As De Beauvoir (1976) explained, "one does not submit to a war or an occupation as he does to an earthquake: he must take sides for or against, and the foreign wills thereby become allied or hostile," and that it is this "interdependence which explains why oppression is possible and why it is hateful" (p. 82). Within an organizational sense, workers can become aligned with organizational power, thus perpetuating management as an ideology. Achieving greater autonomy at work requires overcoming this human dynamic.

It is often said that freedom is a responsibility. This is no less true organizationally than it is civically. Having the ability to determine for oneself what is worthwhile and productive can be daunting. Consequently, not everyone who works in an organization wants autonomy. For some, there is comfort in being told what to do. Subordinating oneself into a collective is one way an individual might attempt to avoid stress. As Ford (2008) explained, "conformity and authoritarianism are...collective strategies for relieving the anxiety that absolute freedom elicits. We willingly exchange our anxiety and freedom for compulsive activity and the answers provided by others" (pp. 15-16). It is worth examining why this might be the case. From early childhood, through education and adolescence, and into adulthood and one's career, people are conditioned to fear being *wrong*. Anytime a person goes outside the protective cover afforded through conformity and compliance, one risks institutional rebuke. For autonomy to be operationally feasible, those working in an organization must transcend the fear of being wrong. This goes beyond a managerial practice of accepting mistakes. As indicated in section three, the spectacle of work is the process in which workers are busy without being productive. It is beneficial to dissect that phenomenon further. Management as an ideology motivates at least some of those under its control to prefer the spectacle of work (which is not productive), to autonomy (which upon execution, might be less productive than something else could have been). In other words, people in this situation find that it is preferable to engage in the wasteful pursuit of a directed activity than to gamble on pursuing a personally defined activity of potential merit. There is no shortcut to overcoming this barrier. Group acceptance has its place. But conformity is the easiest and most shallow way of gaining this acceptance. Such acceptance is little more than bias and prejudice and it is never based on individual merit. Striving for organizational autonomy is beneficial to the individual because it is aligned with one of the principal motivations of humans. Achieving this primary existential aim generates positive externalities for organizations. The ordering here is important. It is being pursued for its liberating effects; organizational power would potentially allow it based on the derivative benefits in terms of performance. Though as pointed out in the critique of organizational power, just because it would be beneficial does not mean that it will be embraced, since control is lost in the process.

Work is not merely a place to earn an income. When employment is reduced to only that, one is alienated from one's labor (intellectually or physically) and effort becomes transactional. In the process, too much of oneself is sacrificed; one's existence is then defined by perpetual waiting, for the evening, weekend, next vacation, or eventual retirement. As presented in section three, *the spectacle of work*, and extended in section four, *devolving slowly*, one is confronted by meaninglessness. This is not only a concern with individual work but can also be applied to the organization itself. Czarniawska (2008) described how "everyday organizing consists of fragmented activities and events, apparently disjointed actions and conversations that seem to have no particular meaning" (p. 33). Such an eventuality is consequential insofar as it is contrary to one of the central existential drives of humanity. As Frankl (1992) explained, "man's search for meaning is the primary motivation in his life and not a 'secondary rationalization' of instinctual drives. This meaning is unique and specific in that it must and can be fulfilled by him alone; only then does it achieve a significance which will satisfy his own *will* to meaning" (p. 105, emphasis in original). But how is meaning created? Meaning creation is abstract and complex, and often it occurs at the subconscious level. Organizational power through management as an ideology attempts to provide those under their employ with a set of meanings which are of benefit to the institution. While one may accept these initially (discussed in section one, *squares in cubes*), as Frankl indicated one's search for meaning is *unique* and *specific*. Authenticity is the process by which one expresses what is personally meaningful, autonomy is what allows one to enact it. Without authenticity one conforms to the meanings proffered by organizations; without autonomy one is subjugated to enacting those organizational meanings through one's work, or pretending to do so through its spectacle. Management as an ideology obfuscates the process through which these organizational meanings are perpetuated. Organizations are the consequence of human activity. They are created and maintained through direct and indirect effort. One does not need to be conscious of one's part for it to be operationally effective. In these respects, organizations can be viewed as sites of socially constructed reality. Berger and Luckmann (1967) provided insight into the human component of such social constructions:

> Social order exists *only* as a product of human activity. No other ontological status may be ascribed to it without hopelessly obfuscating its empirical manifestations. Both in its genesis (social order is the result of past human activity) and its existence in any instant of time (social order exists only and insofar as human activity continues to produce it) it is a human product. (p. 52, emphasis in original)

In terms of their creation and maintenance, organizations require concerted human effort. Organizational power through management as an ideology attempts to steer employees towards the meanings and actions required to perpetuate the organization indefinitely into the future. Understanding this provides insight into how one could modify organizational reality away from subjugation and alienation and towards greater authenticity and autonomy, as the same mechanisms necessary for its maintenance are the ones which enable change. Since organizational reality is a social construction, it is not immutable. The path forward presented here is neither a *movement*, nor a retreat inward. While there are potential benefits to both of those approaches, there are limitations which ultimately make either method ineffective. One might find comfort through making peace with these dynamics, and whereas there are certain benefits to be derived through solace, such an approach does nothing to alter the *status quo*. In fact, such a personal approach is consistent with management as an ideology. The personal approach, while comforting, does not enhance the organizational space for authenticity and autonomy for oneself or one's colleagues. Just as there are limitations associated with a retreat inwards, there are also concerns with a social movement aimed at provoking confrontation with organizational power. First, as Alinsky (1989) explained, revolutionary change must be preceded by a "passive, affirmative, non-challenging attitude toward change among the mass of people. They must feel so frustrated, so defeated, so lost, so futureless in the prevailing system that they are willing to let go of the past and chance the future" (p. xix). Regarding this necessary precondition, the situation is premature for a social movement. Second, social movements are often too utopian for the pragmatic individuals engaged in organizations. Therefore, the critical mass required for galvanized revolution might never be reached. Lastly, utopian movements upon implementation frequently devolve into dystopian nightmares. This last point warrants a little more development. Doing so requires some context as to general characteristics of utopias and dystopias.

Utopias are places of ideal perfection, which are "incongruous with the state of reality within which it occurs" (Mannheim, 1949, p. 173). Predominately, utopian constructions are used for envisioning alternatives to political systems. In this way, utopias offer points of comparison from which one can assess the degree of divergence between a given reality to a theorized ideal. As developed throughout this critique, organizations share common attributes with political systems. First, there are superstructures of power which operate over and around individuals. These structures *seduce* and *coerce* individuals to conform. Second, both systems operate using ideology. As stated in section one, *squares in cubes*, management as an ideology is a form of organizational legitimation, exercised through organizational power, which benefits the system in which the theory and praxis of management is enacted. Lastly, the elements of superstructures of power and ideology combine to engender a sense of helplessness on the part of the individual vis-à-vis the system of subjugation. The individual within organizations is both isolated and overwhelmed. There is a linkage and irresolvable antagonism between utopias and ideology. In some respects, they can be viewed as competing paradigms. As Mannheim explained, "it is always the dominant group which is in full accord with the existing order that determines what is to be regarded as utopian, while the ascendant group which is in conflict with things as they are is the one that determines what is regarded as ideologies" (p. 183). In this way, those subjugated within organizations can point out how policies and institutionalizations are legitimated through and perpetuated by *ideology* and organizational power can dismiss the aspirational suggestions of workers as utopian. It is useful to appreciate that the concept of utopia is not only a form of literature, but that it has already been applied to management (Gibelman, 2004; Nuesiri, 2016; Parker, 1998). The work of Sułkowski (2011) is particularly useful here, as it points to how the "social utopia of management is based on a belief in creating a better social order thanks to employment of the ideas of scientific management" (p. 29), and that there is a "recognition of the significance of utopian thinking in management" (p. 31). As Sułkowski pointed out explicitly, it is not just workers who aspire to something better, but that management itself makes use of utopian thinking. Management as an ideology is utopian as it asserts that through its theory and praxis a *better* society is possible. It is this insight in particular which influenced against this proposed path forward being based on a social movement. If management itself has utopian foundations and motivations, and the issues identified through this critique of organizational power which is enacted through management as an ideology are sufficiently problematic, one can only conclude that there is a high probability that theoretical utopias regarding organizational management become dystopian realities upon implementation. To appreciate this concern more fully it is useful to provide some insight into dystopias.

In contradistinction to utopias, dystopias are frequently portrayed as totalitarian societies of immense human suffering, injustice, and fear. Power is used tyrannically in dystopias by those in elite classes to subjugate a majority of the population. In response to such structural oppression, *resistance* to regimes of totalitarian power is a central component of dystopian fiction. Examples of dystopias are to be found in works of literature including *Brave New World*, *Nineteen Eighty-Four*, *A Clockwork Orange*, and *Fahrenheit 451*, and in works of cinema to include *Idiocracy*, *Escape From New York*, *Planet of the Apes*, and *V for Vendetta*. Dystopian constructions have been applied to management as well (Bray & Thauer, 2016; Burrell & Dale, 2002; Neuman, 1991). Dystopian literature is useful in critiquing organizational power as it reveals in sharp contrast dynamics which are obfuscated by management as ideology. Jackson (2021) explained that "dystopian works....highlight corrosive effects of obedience and conformity," and that what is "of particular importance within an organizational context is the power dynamics between managers and subordinates" which are observable in dystopian works (p. 210). Such dystopian qualities are observable in both particular focus areas and positions. In terms of the focus area of corporate social responsibility (CSR), Bray and Thauer, noted that for those in business and management who deal with CSR may have "utopian hopes, but may also confront a dystopian reality" (p. 278), and that "while pursuing utopian visions... working in the economy of emerging markets is often a dystopia" (p. 281). The work of Bray and Thauer helps in illustrating how utopian ambitions can devolve into dystopian consequences. Again, the path forward presented here is not a social movement due to the likely gap between utopian intent and dystopian effect. Such a dystopian reversal between design and consequence is observable in positions of leadership as well. Jackson, Reboulet, and Bode (2019) described leadership in postmodernity as "a dystopia of crumbling façades and apathy" (p. 59). The notion of *apathy* has been adequately covered throughout this critique. Façades, however, are worthy of a little more development. In architecture, a façade is the outward appearance of a building which is used to maintain and conceal its less pleasing, *structural* features. As an example, many houses within the United States are light frame construction made of timber, with a brick façade. This is different from a brick house which is made of a series of interlocking bricks. The purpose of this example is to highlight a distinction between underlying structure and superficial appearance. This critique of organizational power was designed to expose the façade created and sustained through management as an ideology to reveal its underlying structure of subjugation and alienation. Through the process the individual and organizational need for greater authenticity and autonomy become increasingly apparent.

Prior to progressing further along this path, it is beneficial to summarize some of the key points developed thus far in this section. First, attempts to improve the theory and praxis of management are not new. These attempts largely occur within management as an ideology. Second, organizations are conservative insofar as they are designed to perpetuate the *status quo*. Third, management as an ideology incentivizes competition among peers which precludes the establishment of solidarity aimed at improving general working conditions and labor's share of the surplus value generated within organizations. Fourth, since organizations are socially constructed, they are amenable to being redefined in ways which enhance authenticity and autonomy. Lastly, utopian social movements, however well intentioned, frequently devolve into dystopias upon establishment. Consequently, it is beneficial to contemplate a path forward that does not require a vast social movement, but which also does not simply reside within the minds of individuals. A path forward is needed in which individuals are actively committed to honest collaboration and solidarity, and in which authenticity and autonomy are considered organizational values and are respected as human virtues which are established for each member of the organization regardless of one's employment echelon. The following détournement, *A Path Forward*, provides a point of reflection for moving beyond the subjugation and alienation produced through management as an ideology.

A Path Forward

Confronting the concerns presented in this critique is daunting. As an individual, the challenges may feel insurmountable, but things do not have to stay the way they are currently. Subjugation and alienation are not inevitable. Organizations are human creations and are therefore amenable to modification. Humans have an amazing ability to transform reality. One can take positive actions to make things better for oneself and all those within an organization. Doing so effectively requires an understanding of organizational power and management as an ideology. The détournement, *A Path Forward*, shows an office door opening onto a path in nature. Authenticity is our birthright, our natural state. Each of us exists to define and express our uniqueness. The path forward is one towards greater authenticity and autonomy at work. Moving forward requires the creativity to envision something better and the courage to embark on that path once defined. This is not a utopian movement or a retreat into one's subjectivity. Management as an ideology obfuscates many of the barriers to authenticity and autonomy. As stated throughout this critique, organizational power is a significant force of dressage. Consequently, it is essential to return to the notion of *power* as the essential first step forward.

In the preface to this critique, it was stated that power resides at the core of management theory and praxis. Organizational power has been shown to seduce and constrain individuals resulting in subjugation and alienation. Gaining greater authenticity and autonomy at work requires understanding and overcoming organizational power as enacted through management as an ideology. Power is important, and whereas there is some limited debate as to just how important power is in management, there is general agreement that it is, *in fact*, important. Shoubo Xu and Li Da Xu (2011) contended that "the historical development of human society shows that management is closely related to power. Power is considered the most important factor in management" (p. 54). Their work situates power at the core of management and asserts that power is its most important factor. As such, a focused critique on organizational power is inseparable from an understanding of management as an ideology. For others, power is an important factor for consideration, but not necessarily the most important factor or one that can be examined in isolation. As Dyer (1979) explained, "power is important, and is a factor in understanding behavior. By itself, it is limited in its effectiveness for people in management. There is evidence that mixture of power and caring is important to the ability to influence others" (p. 89). Dyer's point regarding caring will be examined further subsequently in this section. For now, it is sufficient to note that power, even when it is considered to be of only limited effectiveness alone, is still essential enough to be included among the important factors of management theory and praxis. A consequence of management as an ideology is that its unquestioned acceptance allows for management to expand beyond the parameters of an organization. Such an eventuality leads to a similar subjugation in one's personal life as to that experienced professionally. This becomes perhaps even more pressing as the workforce increasingly transitions to working virtually. When this occurs, one could consider it an act of *managementization*. As explained by Maravelias (2011) "managerial authority, in its urge to increase its sway and scope, progresses beyond its traditional and legitimate field of jurisdiction" (p. 105). Organizational power through management as an ideology has the capacity to infiltrate deep into areas once considered to be *personal*. As defined by Maravelias, "the term 'managementization'...refers to how management has overflowed its traditional organizational habitat so that it is now the life of employees that are to be (self) managed for the sake of upholding social, active and flexible selves striving for professional success," and that "managementization implies that attempts to manage individuals who expect and are expected to self-manage their work and life will inescapably be sensitive, in part contradictory, and possibly illegitimate" (p. 107). The border between what is considered by organizations to be personal and what is professional is contestable. Management as an ideology will appropriate as much of the personal sphere as is beneficial to ensure continued subjugation of employees at work. Technological advances enable organizations near constant surveillance of employees, in theory if not yet in practice. This makes staking a claim for greater authenticity and autonomy more important than ever. Doing so effectively requires showing organizational power that more is to be gained through worker autonomy than through the *control* which is asserted as a legitimate function of management.

Increasing globalization has created a chaotic business environment which is volatile, uncertain, complex, and ambiguous. Managing in such an environment is challenging at best. This places stress upon organizational power and management as an ideology. Determining what, if anything, is the *correct* course of action, while facing the constraints of time imposed by global competition, has further exacerbated the task of organizational management. This situation provides one path forward for greater authenticity and autonomy at work. As Kaplan (2019) explained, "businesses face more and more unpredictability that emanates from market volatility, socio-political instability, dramatic weather events, and global interdependence like a Federal Government shutdown, California fires, and cyber attacks. Complexity instills persistent internal uncertainty;" in response to these geopolitical complexities, "adaptability must be a core competence to respond swiftly and astutely to unplanned circumstances...self-managed teams drive improved productivity, customer satisfaction, employee engagement and retention, and innovation" (p. 65). As indicated by Kaplan, the complexities increasingly faced by organizations provide a viable rationale for the use of *self-managed teams*. There are two components to that construction, both warrant some focus. First, the teams are *self-managed*. Autonomy resides at the core of self-management. As discussed previously, autonomy here does not mean that one does whatever is desired, but rather determining and pursuing the directions, tasks, and activities one has determined will be productive and beneficial. Second, the *teams* are self-managed. More will be presented around this concept subsequently, for now it is sufficient to note that teaming provides an opportunity for *collaborative solidarity*. It is in the space provided by collaborative solidarity that one can achieve greater authenticity at work. Together, the complexities faced by modern organizations provide a basis for the enactment of self-managed teams, which could result in a reduction in subjugation and alienation and an increase in authenticity and autonomy. These benefits, while possible, are far from assured. Those seeking greater authenticity and autonomy at work benefit from understanding that obtaining them will come at a price. Most directly autonomy brings with it increased responsibility. Autonomous workers are no longer able to hide behind the directions provided by managers. It is at this point that a philosophical conundrum arises. An authentic person might legitimately eschew autonomy at work. This point is worthy of development.

This critique of organizational power has detailed that management as an ideology contributes to subjugation and alienation of workers and lower-echelon managers. The global economy in which organizations operate creates pressures and constraints which make the adoption of self-managed teams potentially enticing. Through these self-managed teams, greater authenticity and autonomy are possible. Throughout this critique authenticity and autonomy are presented largely in tandem and that workers will desire and benefit from having both. As noted, it is possible that workers expressing their authenticity might not want the autonomy afforded through self-management. While there are a multitude of reasons why this might be the case, the only one focused upon here is stress. A worker might hold a view like, *had I wanted this stress I would have become a manager.* Consequently, one might resist organizational attempts to adopt self-management. Such a situation points to the complexities associated with achieving organizational authenticity. Part of the process of determining what is authentic for an individual, is to distinguish between those aspects of the organization with which one identifies and those with which one does not. As Paulsson (2011) explained, "resistance is part of a dis-identification process, away from, and against, the organization. It has also been suggested that dis-identification processes are part of the production of a new sense of self" (p. 133). Achieving authenticity within an organization requires working through these complexities. As one does, the result might be to authentically resist autonomy. In this regard, Paulsson explained that "self-management can be resisted. It can be resisted as the self-managed workers use the freedom that comes with self-management" (p. 134). The resolution of these complexities occurs within a specific context at the individual level. For the purpose of this critique, it is sufficient to illustrate that the path forward towards greater authenticity and autonomy is not necessarily straightforward. Those who aspire for authenticity and autonomy at work benefit from understanding that one's colleagues may not share all of these same ambitions. Two notions which are essential to this path forward are *care* and *collaborative solidarity.* Organizational power through management as an ideology has relied too long on coercion as the basis for mobilization and action. There is no reason to expect that using those same techniques to overcome organizational power would result in anything other than further subjugation and alienation. With an understanding of these complexities established, it is possible to turn towards a path of greater authenticity and autonomy.

Whereas there are reasons organizations might adopt self-managed teams, autonomy is seldom given. There is nobody from whom one can ask for autonomy without ironically subjugating oneself. Management as an ideology asserts the privilege of control which is exercised through organizational power. If power is viewed as a fixed resource, the more autonomy granted the less power those in upper echelons retain. This is a rather rudimentary understanding of power, and one that is largely rejected in this critique. Even if that view is adopted one can still move forward on a path towards greater authenticity and autonomy. A worker or lower-echelon manager can carve out increasing autonomy by taking personal initiative on projects of perceived value. In the short term, this approach means the individual will be doing more work as one will execute both the self-directed project as well as all organizationally assigned workload. Doing so produces several benefits worthy of consideration. First, one will be *busy* which as we discussed is an organizational preference established through management as an ideology. Second, one provides evidence that one can add organizational value through autonomous work. It is important to understand that freedom is *seized* not given. Be careful here! The organization will likely attempt to seduce an individual showing initiative and adding value into the managerial ranks to move that individual *up* (as well as *away*) and not allow the example of self-management to take root organizationally. The intent of this strategy is to show that management itself is unnecessary, and that autonomy is organizationally productive.

Notice this approach is indirect. In general, don't attack the system directly as organizational power will mobilize a defense; rather, make a given target area irrelevant. As indicated, there will be those who for a variety of reasons choose to advance through the managerial ranks rather than struggle for greater authenticity and autonomy at work. A strategy of collaborative solidarity should be used with these colleagues. People have different talents, understandings, inclinations, ambitions, needs, and fears. People with whom one disagrees are not necessarily one's *enemy*. The shared enemy of both is usually those who wish to preclude understanding and authentic, collegial, productive debate on issues of merit through obfuscation. Organizational power through management as an ideology obfuscates and manipulates; it is therefore a legitimate target worthy of critique. The path to authenticity and autonomy rests on collaborative solidarity and care. As such, each of these elements requires some development to enable one to embrace them as organizational tactics.

Think of a victor in a competition. Now think of a compassionate person assisting somebody in need. Which situation provides a richer sense of accomplishment? While there are certainly variations among people, often the thrill of victory is transitory whereas the joy of making another person's life better is lasting. Management as an ideology encourages competition throughout organizations. One is in a state of perpetual competition with one's peers for raises and advancement. Under such a construction one is willing to help another only insofar as it is not detrimental to one's professional prospects. These inclinations are formed over a lifetime. From youth, the games played groom all those engaged towards developing a competitive spirit. The rules of these games instruct us to desire winning and, more importantly, to not be a sore loser. This is not random. Games are used to instruct children on the rules beneficial to those in power within the society in which they live. In an economic system which requires a competitive spirit for advancement, but also one that generates innumerably more losers than it does winners, the rules of the games played need to incentivize winning as a means of obtaining personal glory, just as they require the losers to graciously accept defeat and admire, rather than begrudge, the few who win. The games of one's youth prepare one for the realities one will face as an adult. In a game victory provides a sense of elation, but professionally *winning* in such a system doesn't provide a lasting sense of accomplishment. Being slightly better off than the mass of people struggling around oneself can be a source of embarrassment rather than pride. Through experience and dressage, one learns to be competitive and apathetic. Part of gaining authenticity is to assess the degree to which the very things one thinks one desires have been socially and organizationally manufactured and are contrary to what enriches one's life. Collaborative solidarity is both a cause and consequence of authenticity. Collaboration is the act of working with someone to create something of value; solidarity is a feeling of unity among a group of individuals with a common interest. Collaborative solidarity combines the *actions* of collaboration with the *feelings* of solidarity. Both are important for achieving greater authenticity and autonomy.

Organizational power through management as an ideology attempts to make itself the focus of unity. While perpetually infinite, organizations are abstractions. The *real* organization, for those working within, is one's colleagues. Anybody returning to an old school after several years away has experienced the strange sensation of familiarity and estrangement. All the rooms remain the same, but the feelings are different. It isn't the same. One finds that it was largely one's friends and teachers who made the memorable moments, not the buildings. Management as an ideology obfuscates this. Admittedly, organizations are designed to function independent of specific people. Over the course of many years, people come, and people go. Management as an ideology latches on to this transitoriness in personnel and attempts to convince workers that this means the organization and not the people should be the focus of unity. Nothing could be further from the truth. While the people who happen to inhabit an organization are to a degree random, once they are selected, they are the ones who *specifically* make the organization. Once the specific individuals are selected, one could keep those people, switch the organizational logo on their coffee mugs, and not much about the functioning of the office would change. Collaborative solidarity provides appropriate focus on the specific individuals with whom one shares work and a significant portion of one's life. It is through collaborative solidarity that authenticity has its most rewarding application. At an extreme, authenticity could mean letting one's *freak flag fly*. There is certainly joy in embracing freely the fullness of one's existence. Within collaborative solidarity a somewhat narrower authenticity is envisioned; one in which the pretenses associated with professionalism are abandoned. In this way, one is free to be imperfect, unknowing, and vulnerable. This authenticity provides many benefits individually and organizationally. Only a few will be mentioned. First, being authentic provides possible points of real connection with one's colleagues. Second, it provides more accurate information which allows existing gaps in understandings and skills to be more quickly identified and addressed, Third, one is liberated from the fear of being *found out*. Lastly, the energy which was being expended on maintaining and projecting one's façade can be redirected towards one's work or developing those benefiting from personal investment. In addition to the benefits listed already, authenticity provides a basis for *care*.

As previously referenced, Dyer (1979) recommended combining power with care to influence more effectively the members of organizations. Incorporating care with the use of power certainly seemingly humanizes the application of organizational power and is potentially more effective. Essentially, incorporating care with power is ultimately still using power as a means of coercion. Whereas Dyer suggests a pragmatic utility associated with using care as a means to an end, the place for care individually and organizationally is arguably even more essential than a mere organizational tactic. In fact, care can be placed at the center of existential being. Such a placement of care is most prominent in the work of Heidegger (1962). For Heidegger, being-in-the-world must be "interpreted in terms of the phenomenon of *care*" (p. 157, emphasis in original). In fact, care is how existential being is ultimately defined. What does Heideggerian care mean? As Heidegger explained, "in care is grounded the full diclosedness [*sic*] of the 'there'" (p. 402). Consistent with this existential construction, care can be defined beneficially within an organizational context as being present in one's professional activities. This has direct application to alienation. As indicated throughout this critique, the spectacle of work results in alienation. Care provides an effective antidote to this alienation. The care envisioned here is not some *mushy* sentiment, but rather a personal presence in the activities in which one is engaged. Care, in this sense, is closely related to professional integrity and reflects a personal investment in what one is doing. Being present professionally through care isn't only about one's relationship with tasks but is also to be established in one's relationships with others. In its interpersonal application, care requires being present to the authentic being and needs of others. In fact, one could argue that care is essential for the collaborative solidarity previously presented. Care for one's colleagues requires replacing superficiality, pretense, and phoniness with depth, authenticity, and sincerity.

Implementing collaborative solidarity and care requires overcoming some personal and organizational barriers, starting with the investment in time and attention required for these to be real rather than rhetorical. Again, what is proposed here isn't a social movement or an improvement program. These suggestions are meant as personal commitments which hold the potential to increase authenticity and autonomy for oneself and others. Just as with anything worthwhile, it will only materialize after concerted effort. Additionally, for collaborative solidarity and care to take hold, one must overcome much of the perspectives and expectations provided subconsciously through the unquestioned acceptance of management as an ideology. This critique of organizational power highlighted just a few of the major elements (e.g., being busy, competition). As such, this is only a starting point for one's inquiry and reflection. Establishing authenticity requires one to interrogate both *what* one thinks and *why* one thinks it. One will likely find through the process that much of what one thinks rests on a foundation of nothing more than some person with some degree of authority said *it* when one was young. Much of organizational subjugation rests on similarly flimsy foundations. Lastly, a renewed sense of respect and empathy needs to be cultivated. In a society and organizations which valorize wealth, success, and power, it is relatively easy to marginalize people who have little of those attributes. When engaged in perpetual competition, from a precarious situation, it is difficult to imagine how or why one would make time for assisting those who couldn't possibly contribute to one's own advancement. As asserted at the beginning of this critique, all people and all work have inherent dignity. Along the path towards greater authenticity and autonomy is the awareness that collaborative solidarity and care are enriching. By engaging with each other in this way one breaks free from the subjugation and alienation which are unavoidable through management as an ideology. Further, unless one is to be hypocritical, to want these things for oneself is to want them for all others. As Sartre (2007) explained:

> When I affirm that freedom under any concrete circumstance, can have no other aim than itself, and once a man realizes, in his state of abandonment, that it is he who imposes values, he can will but one thing: freedom as the foundation of all values...in thus willing, we discover that it depends on the freedom of others, and that the freedom of others depends on my own...I cannot set my own freedom as a goal without also setting the freedom of others as a goal (pp. 48-49)

Authenticity and autonomy are virtues which, like freedom, require them to be goals which one demands for all those within an organization if one is to have them securely established for oneself. As revealed through this critique, management as an ideology establishes subjugation and alienation as the collective universal aims of organizational power. One is encouraged to examine the situation as objectively as possible and determine what is best for oneself.

In forecasting, one benefits from maintaining the humility of probabilities rather than the arrogance of certainties. Making sense of one's situation is complex. Determining what to do is seldom easy. People are largely muddling through (Lindblom, 1959). Events which seem nearly certain are routinely avoided through human courage and creativity; events which are highly unlikely occur all around us. No situation, no matter how dire it may be predicted to be, or how likely its forecasted probability, is fully set in stone while it remains to be enacted. It is useful as well to appreciate that while some aspects of the future are pure chance, other aspects are amenable to human intervention. There is always space in which one can hope and dedicate effort to improve the realized outcome. This hope, if it is to be pragmatically active, benefits from being grounded in a realistic appraisal of the situation, and not an escape from an unpleasant reality into a preferred fantasy. This critique of organizational power has continually pointed to subjugation and alienation as consequences of management as an ideology. What is the logical conclusion along that path? The United States is on an economic course the trajectory of which seems destined to culminate with oligarchs and organizational serfs, with some technocrats existing in the chasm between the two. A 2020 Pew Research report found that the share of U.S. aggregate income held by those in the middle-income group has declined from 61% in 1971 to 51% in 2019. The middle-class in the United States is shrinking. In the words of Yeats, *things fall apart; the centre cannot hold; mere anarchy is loosed upon the world.* For those who see a strong middle class as contributing to the strength and stability of the United States, such a decline is concerning. Economic consequences created through management as an ideology are worth considering, but so too are its existential consequences.

Management as an ideology produces inferior substitutes which impoverish our existential well-being in turn for only meager economic compensation. Through the process superficial politeness replaces collegiality, busyness replaces productivity, and pay replaces fulfillment. Organizational power creates policies which preclude openness among workers. As one simple example illustrates, organizations routinely prohibit employees from discussing their salaries with each other. The reasoning for such an organizational policy is clear. When people find out that there is a spectrum of wages for the same work this will first engender discord and subsequently result in demands for the higher wage. Such an eventuality holds the potential to do two things, both of which organizations wish to avoid. First, it would result in a larger expense for labor. Second, it would unify workers in solidarity against the upper echelons of an organization. Organizational power creates the policies, and they create the policies which protect and sustain their interests and are beneficial to the system, not its workers. Illusions are only effective for so long. Workers and lower-echelon managers are starting to sense that there is something more than what is obtained through management as an ideology. Through this emerging consciousness there is a heartfelt desire for something real and meaningful. The spectacle of work simply doesn't deliver the goods. Creating the space in which authenticity and autonomy are respected and encouraged could engender a more equitable distribution of the gains from labor; however, the mindset must precede the action (Alinsky, 1989). Ideally, it has become clear that this critique of organizational power is not anti-managers. Lower-echelon managers often inhabit positions which are every bit as subjugating and alienating as those inhabited by workers. Management as an ideology has contributed to the spectacle of work and is instrumental in the organizational implementation of subjugation and alienation, which makes it a barrier to collective solidarity and care and ultimately authenticity and autonomy. Given the seriousness of these concerns and the consequences produced, the key question becomes: under what circumstances and to what degree are the functions of management required to be embodied in a single individual? There is no general answer available to this question. The answer needs to be determined within the specific context of organizations. Whereas the answers depend on context, the question is important enough that it should be asked broadly and frequently. As authenticity, autonomy, collaborative solidary, and care increase within organizations their combined effect will erode the perceived need for the embodiment of managerial functions in a single individual. Perhaps the evidence will eventually be compelling enough that even organizational power will have to acknowledge it.

The economic and existential consequences of management as an ideology warrant scrutiny. This critique of organizational power has identified subjugation and alienation as key elements worthy of consideration. There are admittedly others. Those who have found this critique useful are encouraged to extend its scope in terms of both elements of critique and contexts. In that way, all those engaged in research and action along this path are in collaborative solidarity with each other. Through collaborative solidarity and care greater authenticity and autonomy is possible. Management as an ideology offers a path towards subjugation and alienation, along which workers attempting to avoid these are seduced into management. Upon entering the lower echelons of management one not only discovers more of the same subjugation and alienation but has the compounding effect associated with being the body and voice of its organizational enactment. In response, some attempt to escape into the spectacle of work in which the appearance of being busy replaces productivity. When extended over the course of a career this results in nihilism and burnout. Management as an ideology masks this from those within organizations for the benefit of organizational power. Since organizations are social constructions, they can be redefined based on current needs and demands. A path forward exists. How much longer shall subjugation and alienation be the consequence for one's work? Collaborative solidarity and care within organizations are long overdue. It is possible to move towards authenticity and autonomy at work. With these concepts you can create a path forward that is authentic, collaborative, and fulfilling for yourself and caring towards all those questioning, confronting, and contending with organizational power.

Key Concepts

- Care
- Collaborative solidarity
- Dystopia
- Fulfillment
- Passion
- Utopia

Reflection Questions

1. If you were tasked with developing a better way to execute work, what elements of the traditional management structure would you change? What elements would you retain? How would managers respond to this new system? How would workers respond?
2. Management contains a variety of functions, including administration, planning, and resourcing. What benefits are derived from having some, most, or all these functions executed by a single individual? What benefits are derived from having some, most, or all these functions executed collaboratively?
3. As discussed, there are potentially different motivations behind pursuing a managerial position. Among common motivations are increases in salary and prestige. How would the enactment of management change if there was no increase in pay, and taking the position was viewed as a duty one assumes temporarily for the organization?
4. Management is invested with organizational power. For whom is this investment beneficial? More specifically, does it seem

the current approach to management primarily benefits those in the upper or lower echelons of organizations? If the management functions were shared collaboratively by those at the working level, would this be inherently threatening to those in power? Why or why not?

5. Whether in sports or academics, you have likely worked on teams. Select a team with which you are familiar. Using the concepts of collaborative solidarity and care describe your interactions on the team. Of the two elements, collaborative solidarity, and care, which do consider to be more important to team success? Why did you select that element? Did other team members have the same level of investment?
6. This critique positions subjugation and alienation on one end, and authenticity and autonomy on opposite ends of a spectrum. However, reducing subjugation and alienation is a necessary but not a sufficient condition for having greater authenticity and autonomy. How would you propose increasing the degree of authenticity and autonomy at work?

Epilogue: Towards Authenticity & Autonomy

Language shapes and constrains understanding and action. The power of words can be observed and understood through an examination of the use of slogans in both product commercials and political campaigns. Protests too hold the potential to galvanize thought. Distilling a complex idea effectively so it can be placed on a placard, requires capturing its essence. In a somewhat lengthy protest poster from the 1960s, it was asserted that, *A revolution is not a spectacle! There are no spectators! Everyone participates whether they know it or not.* The takeaway from this is that as one ignores what is going on, one perpetuates the *status quo*. Lack of engagement is a consequential stance. Taking this as a starting point, one might create a spectrum of engagement moving from active resistance on one extreme to active support on the other. In between those two poles are the positions of passive resistance and passive support. In terms of management as an ideology, movements like Occupy Wall Street likely represent active resistance, whereas movements like the Tea Party might represent active support. Whereas each of these movements was large enough to warrant sustained media coverage, people working in offices frequently find themselves somewhere in between these extremes. For many the aim of employment is simply to make a meaningful contribution through the honest execution of their chosen profession, to achieve a comfortable standard of living based on a reasonable assessment of the value of one's labor, and to be able to take some time off to enjoy life as one works. These people likely offer passive support to management as an ideology. In some ways, this critique is targeted primarily to these individuals, as they are likely the most numerous and they are the ones who hold the greatest potential for improving the current situation for themselves and others. Doing so effectively requires a pragmatic vision of a workable alternative.

Unfettered inspiration can spiral into fantasy. When the object of focus is the reformation of a given social order, the specific fiction becomes *utopian*. In general, utopias suffer from a series of fatal flaws. First, they tend to be so far removed from any semblance of reality that practically minded people shrug at the irrelevance of the vision. Second, utopias tend to neglect the human tendencies which contributed to the current reality. Third, by their very nature, utopias are singular, monolithic constructions. Lastly, when enacted utopias can become dystopian in their consequence. Risks abound. A rash imprudence could create chaos resulting in something worse than what currently exists. A stoic reserve will assuredly sustain the barely tolerable *status quo*. Between these two extremes, what is one to do? Once again sayings from the late 1960s provide timely insight. Doing nothing is a *cop out*. The twin tyranny of alienation and subjugation is inherent in the current, common construction of management as an ideology. In the pursuit of greater authenticity and autonomy at work, *it is better to try and fail than to fail to try.* The current situation calls for action grounded in human experience and organizational reality. Quality of life is not an esoteric concern. People trapped in drudgery and fear long for something better. To achieve organizational authenticity and autonomy for oneself, one must respect it for all others. Renewed civility will be needed to disagree productively on substantive issues. This can be achieved by focusing on our shared humanity and search for meaning, in collaborative solidarity and with care.

Humans have inherent dignity, as does the work that they do, individually and collectively. Any work, at any level, can be ennobling and a source of pride. Management as an ideology blinds one to this. Through the dressage of organizational power, collective focus is directed towards ever greater advancement, prestige, power, and wealth. There isn't anything inherently wrong with those things. In fact, the drive for career achievements can be a source of great pride and satisfaction. It is only when the pursuit of these things becomes myopic, unquestioned, and facilitates the marginalization of others that it becomes a social problem worthy of critique. What one does and how one does it matter. Work is consequential. How that work is directed and orchestrated also matters. Structurally, management as an ideology creates a hierarchy of status and privilege. Management is nothing if it is not the sanctioned, cascading, subordination of the relative valuation of work within an organization. Work enacted at higher echelons is viewed as *strategic* and resting on the unique qualities of the individual holding the position, whereas work at lower echelons is viewed as *tactical* and easily replaceable by anybody who happens to hold the position at a given point in time. Within management as an ideology, one's work is easily and routinely trivialized. One becomes alienated from the product of one's labor. Managers too are affected, especially those at lower echelons, as agency is surrendered to give voice and embodiment to corporate positions. Reimagining this dynamic holds potential for enriched individual and collective action.

Existentially, of course, we remain alone. The weight of individuality is inescapable. Paradoxically, work can simultaneously reduce and enhance feelings of isolation. Being part of an organization holds the potential to establish shared meanings and connections. Through common goals a unity of purpose can be achieved which provides one with a sense of belonging. Executing work to which one is increasingly divorced can intensify a sense of separation. The spectacle of work is alienating. One's occupation often is part of how one comes to understand and define oneself. Where one works, what one does, and how the work is managed each play a part. In the construction of identity, work matters. The critique of organizational power presented here has focused on authenticity and autonomy as essential to personal and professional fulfillment through work. These concepts are vital to individual empowerment. As important as they are individually, it is important to consider that work, at its best, is more than a collection of individuals. People can unite and encourage each other. Authentic connection is possible between colleagues. Collaborative solidarity is achievable. One can care about the work and each other. Management as an ideology obfuscates this by subordinating everything to profit, market share, and mission. It is worth considering to what degree the current approach to management hinders the enriching outcomes of authenticity, autonomy, and collegiality. Through this critique the position has been staked that working more authentically with greater autonomy requires overcoming, or at a minimum redirecting, the dressage of organizational power. It is worth repeating that the characteristics management as an ideology promotes for workers are those which are beneficial to the organization and not those which are enriching for the individual. When the two align it is mere happenstance, not by design.

Organizational power is exerted directly in how one dresses, what one says, and where and when one is allowed to engage in nonwork activities occurring during business hours (e.g., taking a break or having lunch). Indirectly, organizational power can even influence the types of activities in which one engages, the degree of one's political involvement, and how freely one talks about work and oneself. Organizational power is routinized, controlling, and limiting. To be *in the system*, one gives up elements of *oneself*. When one needs a job, it is understandable that security and paychecks are worth conformity. The focus of this critique isn't on the rational, individual decision to make this choice, but rather on the system which necessitates making it. Stifling conformity is seldom a path for creativity. Authenticity and autonomy are key elements of empowerment and progress. The degree to which the organizational approach to management enhances authenticity and autonomy, and the degree to which individuals embrace these elements are key components to quality, for both organizational performance and life.

This critique addressed the quandary of management. *Squares in cubes* (section one), focused on management from a subordinate's perspective, *the unbearable banality of management* (section two), examined management as experienced from a manager's perspective, *the spectacle of work* (section three) brought attention to the performative aspects of employment, *devolving slowly* (section four) focused on the entropic nature of sustaining the spectacle over a prolonged period, and lastly, *a path forward* (section five), provided an alternative to the current construction of management. Collectively, this critique of organizational power points to the subjugation and alienation which are consequences of management as an ideology and identifies the need for greater authenticity and autonomy. Too many work in an endless abyss of existential drudgery. This chasm is of human creation. Fixing it is within our grasp, individually and collectively. What can one do to maintain organizational performance as one engages in disrupting the *status quo* perpetuated through management as ideology? This critique of organizational power presented aspects of the situation, along with thoughts related to an alternative, to contribute another voice to the ongoing discussion. Traditional management offers a path towards subjugation and alienation. Constructing a path forward is *pivotal*, both in terms of it being crucially important and as it provides a fixed point around which subsequent actions are possible. Modernizing management requires its deconstruction as an ideology to align with the human needs of authenticity and autonomy. This is long overdue. We need to move beyond the lethargy of passive acceptance of the *status quo*. It is time to join the prolonged struggle for greater authenticity and autonomy at work.

References

Al Shamsi, I. R. (2020). Business Typology for Examining the Risk Management Strategy in Relation to the Activities of Higher Education Institutions in the Sultanate of Oman. *TEM Journal*, *9*(2), 722–730. https://doi.org/10.18421/tem92-40

Alinsky, S. D. (1989). *Rules for radicals: A pragmatic primer for realistic radicals*. Vintage Books.

Althusser, L. (2014). *On the reproduction of capitalism: Ideology and Ideological State Apparatuses*. Verso.

Angelova, J. (2019). Market Model for Management of Profit in Industrial Enterprise. *Trakia Journal of Sciences*, *17*(Supplement 1), 606–610. https://doi.org/10.15547/tjs.2019.s.01.096

Argyris, C. (1998). Managers, Workers, and Organizations. *Society*, *35*(2), 343–346. https://doi.org/10.1007/BF02838160

Azambuja, R., & Islam, G. (2019). Working at the boundaries: Middle managerial work as a source of emancipation and alienation. *HUMAN RELATIONS*, *72*(3), 534–564. https://doi.org/10.1177/0018726718785669

Barnes-Farrell, J. L., Rumery, S. M., & Swody, C. A. (2002). How Do Concepts of Age Relate to Work and Off-the-Job Stresses and Strains? A Field Study of Health Care Workers in Five Nations. *Experimental Aging Research*, *28*(1), 87–98. https://doi.org/10.1080/036107302753365577

Bartley, T., Soener, M., & Gershenson, C. (2019). Power at a distance: Organizational power across boundaries. *Sociology Compass*, *13*(10). https://doi.org/10.1111/soc4.12737

Baudrillard, J. (1994). *Simulacra and simulation*. The University of Michigan Press.

Berger, P. L., & Luckmann, T. (1967). *The social construction of reality: A treatise in the sociology of knowledge*. Anchor Books.

Berthung, E., Gutacker, N., Friborg, O., Abelsen, B., & Olsen, J. A. (2021). Who keeps on working? The importance of resilience for labour market participation. *PLoS ONE*, *16*(10), 1–10. https://doi.org/10.1371/journal.pone.0258444

Berti, M., & Simpson, A. V. (2021). The Dark Side of Organizational Paradoxes: The Dynamics of Disempowerment. *Academy of Management Review*, *46*(2), 252–274. https://doi.org/10.5465/amr.2017.0208

Bohórquez Arévalo, L. E. (2016). The absence of response of organizations to changing business environment conditions: a complex management problem. *Pensamiento & Gestión*, *41*, 13–35.

Braverman, H. (1974). *Labor and monopoly capital: The degradation of work in the twentieth century*. Monthly Review Press.

Bray, Z., & Thauer, C. (2016). Utopian Spaces, Dystopian Places? A Local Community-Based Perspective on Corporate Social Responsibility. *Nature & Culture*, *11*(3), 278–295. https://doi.org/10.3167/nc.2016.110304

Brennan, D., & Wendt, L. (2021). Increasing Quality and Patient Outcomes with Staff Engagement and Shared Governance. *Online Journal of Issues in Nursing, 26*(2), N.PAG. https://doi.org/10.3912/ojin.vol26no02ppt23

Burrell, G., & Dale, K. (2002). Utopiary: Utopias, gardens and organization. Sociological Review. Monograph, 50(2), 106-127. https://doi.org/10.1111/j.1467-954X.2002.tb03581.x

Buzády, Z., & Georgiu, A. (2011). Riding the Waves of the Motivation Cycle. *OD Practitioner, 43*(1), 35–41.

Camus, A. (1991). *The myth of Sisyphus and other essays.* Vintage Books.

Collins, M. E., Block, S. D., Arnold, R. M., & Christakis, N. A. (2009). On the prospects for a blame-free medical culture. *Social Science & Medicine, 69*(9), 1287–1290. https://doi.org/10.1016/j.socscimed.2009.08.033

Cordes, C. L., Dougherty, T. W., & Blum, M. (1997). Patterns of Burnout among Managers and Professionals: A Comparison of Models. *Journal of Organizational Behavior, 18*(6), 685–701.

Curcuruto, M., & Griffin, M. A. (2018). Prosocial and proactive "safety citizenship behaviour" (SCB): The mediating role of affective commitment and psychological ownership. *Safety Science, 104*, 29–38. https://doi.org/10.1016/j.ssci.2017.12.010

Czarniawska, B. (2008). *A theory of organizing.* Edward Elgar.

De Beauvoir, S. (1976). *The ethics of ambiguity.* Citadel Press.

Debord, G. (2005). *Society of the spectacle.* Black & Red.

Deem, R., & Brehony, K. J. (2005). Management as ideology: the case of 'new managerialism' in higher education. *Oxford Review of Education, 31*(2), 217–235.

Demirci, A. E. (2019). Organizational Culture and Management Cynicism: How Different Cultural Profiles Affect Cynical Views on Managers. *Anadolu University Journal of Social Sciences*, *19*(3), 305–320. https://doi.org/10.18037/ausbd.632108

Donovan, A. M., & Rapp, D. N. (2020). Look it up: Online search reduces the problematic effects of exposures to inaccuracies. *Memory & Cognition*, *48*(7), 1128–1145. https://doi.org/10.3758/s13421-020-01047-z

Dyer, W. (1979). Caring and Power. *California Management Review*, *21*(4), 84–89. https://doi.org/10.2307/41164838

Eiser, B. J. A. (2008). In focus/emerging leaders: Meeting the challenge of moving from technical expert to leader. *Leadership in Action*, *28*(5), 13–24. https://doi.org/10.1002/lia.1262

Elgammal, A., Turetken, O., Heuvel, W.-J., & Papazoglou, M. (2016). Formalizing and appling compliance patterns for business process compliance. *Software & Systems Modeling*, *15*(1), 119–146. https://doi.org/10.1007/s10270-014-0395-3

Elgharbawy, A., & Abdel-Kader, M. (2021). Value-Based Management, Corporate Governance and Organizational Performance: Evidence from the Uk. *Journal of Developing Areas*, *55*(2), 115–130. https://doi.org/10.1353/jda.2021.0035

Figueredo, J.-M., García-Ael, C., Gragnano, A., & Topa, G. (2021). The Mediating Role of Work-Health Balance in the Relationship between Perceived Work Ability and Affective Job Satisfaction. *Psihologijske Teme / Psychological Topics*, *30*(3), 547–572. https://doi.org/10.31820/pt.30.3.8

Fine, S., & Pirak, M. (2016). Faking Fast and Slow: Within-Person Response Time Latencies for Measuring Faking in Personnel Testing. *Journal of Business & Psychology, 31*(1), 51–64. https://doi.org/10.1007/s10869-015-9398-5

Fisher, R. (2007). Putting the "Team" in the Fine Arts Team: An Application of Business Management Team Concepts. *Arts Education Policy Review, 108*(4), 25–32. https://doi.org/10.3200/AEPR.108.4.25-32

Ford, D. (2008). *The search for meaning.* University of California Press.

Foucault, M. (1980). *Power/Knowledge: Selected interviews & other writings 1972-1977.* Pantheon Books.

Fournier, V., & Smith, W. (2012). Making choice, taking risk: On the coming out of Critical Management Studies. *Ephemera: Theory & Politics in Organization, 12*(4), 463–474.

Frankl, V. (1992). *Man's search for meaning.* Beacon Press.

Gibelman, M. (2004). Searching for Utopia: The Cycles of Service Provider Preference. *Administration in Social Work, 28*(3/4), 137–159. https://doi.org/10.1300/J147v28n03_07

Graves, L., & Luciano, M. (2013). Self-determination at work: Understanding the role of leader-member exchange. *Motivation & Emotion, 37*(3), 518–536. https://doi.org/10.1007/s11031-012-9336-z

Green, C. (2013). The organizational power matrix: Toward a Metapraxis of Power. *Journal of Integral Theory & Practice, 8*(1/2), 87–105.

Halldorsdottir, S., Einarsdottir, E. J., & Edvardsson, I. R. (2018). Effects of cutbacks on motivating factors among nurses in primary health care. *Scandinavian Journal of Caring Sciences, 32*(1), 397–406. https://doi.org/10.1111/scs.12474

Hana, U., & Lucie, V. (2015). Investigating Talent Management Philosophies. *Journal of Competitiveness*, *7*(3), 3–18. https://doi.org/10.7441/joc.2015.03.01

Hauk, N., Göritz, A. S., & Krumm, S. (2019). The mediating role of coping behavior on the age-technostress relationship: A longitudinal multilevel mediation model. *PLoS ONE*, *14*(3), 1–22. https://doi.org/10.1371/journal.pone.0213349

Heidegger, M. (1962). *Being and time.* Harper & Row, Publishers, Incorporated.

Hodson, R. (1996). Dignity in the workplace under participative management: Alienation and freedom revisited. *American Sociological Review*, *61*(5), 719–738. https://doi.org/10.2307/2096450

Honda, S., Yanagi, Y., Koizumi, H., Chen, Y., Tanaka, S., Arimoto, M., & Imai, K. (2021). Impact of neovascular age-related macular degeneration: burden of patients receiving therapies in Japan. *Scientific Reports*, *11*(1), 1–9. https://doi.org/10.1038/s41598-021-92567-4

Hovbrandt, P., Håkansson, C., Albin, M., Carlsson, G., & Nilsson, K. (2019). Prerequisites and driving forces behind an extended working life among older workers. *Scandinavian Journal of Occupational Therapy*, *26*(3), 171–183. https://doi.org/10.1080/11038128.2017.1409800

Hudon, P., & Rouillard, C. (2015). Critical Management Studies and public administration: Reinterpreting democratic governance using critical theory and poststructuralism. *Canadian Public Administration*, *58*(4), 527–548. https://doi.org/10.1111/capa.12132

Hummel, R. P. (2008). *The bureaucratic experience: The post-modern challenge.* M. E. Sharpe.

Irving, K. J. (2004). Administering Peace by Managing Integrity: U.N. Peacekeeping Mission Leadership and Evolving Public Administration Theory. *Conference Papers -- American Political Science Association*, 1–25. https://doi.org/apsa_proceeding_28592.pdf

Jackson, R. (2016). The spectacle of analysis: Analytics as organizational propaganda. *ETC: A Review of General Semantics, 73*(4), 355-371.

Jackson, R. (2021). Becoming who you are through authentic organizational communication. In R. Jackson & A. Reboulet (Eds.), *Effective Strategies for Communicating Insights in Business* (pp. 207-222). IGI Global. https://doi.org/10.4018/978-1-7998-3964-4.ch013

Jackson, R. A., & Reboulet, A. M. (2019). Nietzsche's constructions of power: Implications for international business ethics. *International Journal of Responsible Leadership and Ethical Decision-Making, 1*(2), 27-43. https://doi.org/10.4018/IJRLEDM.2019070103

Jackson, R., Reboulet, A., & Bode, T. (2019). *Leadership in postmodernity: A dystopia of crumbling façades and apathy.* Journal of Leadership Studies, 13(1), 59-61.

Kane-Urrabazo, C. (2006). Management's role in shaping organizational culture. *Journal of Nursing Management (Wiley-Blackwell), 14*(3), 188–194. https://doi.org/10.1111/j.1365-2934.2006.00590.x

Kaplan, M. J. (2019). The Imperative for Adaptive Organizations: Is Self-Management a Viable Model? *Organization Development Review, 51*(2), 63–65.

Khaltar, O., & Moon, M. J. (2020). Effects of Ethics and Performance Management on Organizational Performance in the Public Sector. *Public*

Integrity, *22*(4), 372–394. https://doi.org/10.1080/10999922.2019.1615163

Korman, J. V., Van Quaquebeke, N., & Troester, C. (2021). Managers are Less Burned-Out at the Top: The Roles of Sense of Power and Self-Efficacy at Different Hierarchy Levels. *Journal of Business Psychology*. https://doi.org/10.1007/s10869-021-09733-8

Kras, K. R., Portillo, S., & Taxman, F. S. (2017). Managing from the Middle: Frontline Supervisors and Perceptions of Their Organizational Power. *Law and Policy*, *39*(3), 215–236.

Lakoff, G., & Johnson, M. (2003). *Metaphors we live by*. The University of Chicago Press.

Lam, C., & Campbell, K. S. (2021). Follow the Leader? The Impact of Leader Rapport Management on Social Loafing. *Business & Professional Communication Quarterly*, *84*(3), 181–204.

Lewis, B. J. (1999). Surefire Methods of Undermining Teamwork. *Journal of Management in Engineering*, *15*(6), 9.

Lim, V. K. G., Teo, T. S. H., & Loo, G. L. (2002). How Do I Loaf Here? Let Me Count the Ways. *Communications of the ACM*, *45*(1), 66–70. https://doi.org/10.1145/502269.502300

Lindblom, C. E. (1959). The Science of "Muddling Through." *Public Administration Review*, *19*(2), 79–88. https://doi.org/10.2307/973677

Lohela-Karlsson, M., Nybergh, L., & Jensen, I. (2018). Perceived health and work-environment related problems and associated subjective production loss in an academic population. *BMC Public Health*, *18*, 257. https://doi.org/10.1186/s12889-018-5154-x

Lount Jr., R. B., & Wilk, S. L. (2014). Working Harder or Hardly Working? Posting Performance Eliminates

Social Loafing and Promotes Social Laboring in Workgroups. *Management Science*, *60*(5), 1098–1106. https://doi.org/10.1287/mnsc.2013.1820

Lyotard, J.-F. (1984). *The postmodern condition: A report on Knowledge*. University of Minnesota Press.

Mannheim, K. (1949). *An ideology and utopia: An introduction to the sociology of knowledge*. Harcourt, Brace and Company.

Maravelias, C. (2011). The managementization of everyday life -- Work place health promotion and the management of self-managing employees. *Ephemera: Theory & Politics in Organization*, *11*(2), 105–121.

Marcuse, H. (1969). *An essay on liberation*. Beacon Press.

Martin, C. J. (2015). The Effects of Nurse Staffing on Quality of Care. *MEDSURG Nursing*, *24*(2), 4–6.

Martinussen, P. E., & Davidsen, T. (2021). "Professional-supportive" versus "economic-operational" management: the relationship between leadership style and hospital physicians' organisational climate. *BMC Health Services Research*, *21*(1), 1–11. https://doi.org/10.1186/s12913-021-06760-2

Matthews, L., Beeler, L., Zablah, A. R., & Hair, J. F. (2018). All autonomy is not created equal: the countervailing effects of salesperson autonomy on burnout. *Journal of Personal Selling & Sales Management*, *38*(3), 303–322.

Middaugh, D. (2018). Managerial Burnout: Putting Out the Flames. *MEDSURG Nursing*, *27*(2), 121–122.

Mintzberg, H. (1971). Managerial Work: Analysis from Observation. *Management Science*, *18*(2), B97–B110.

Moeini, M., & Rivard, S. (2019). Responding—Or Not—To Information Technology Project Risks: An Integrative

Model. *MIS Quarterly*, *43*(2), 475–500. https://doi.org/10.25300/MISQ/2019/14505

Morrison, J. L., Oladunjoye, G. T., & Onyefulu, C. (2007). An Assessment of Research Supervision: A Leadership Model Enhancing Current Practices in Business and Management. *Journal of Education for Business*, *82*(4), 212–219. https://doi.org/10.3200/JOEB.82.4.212-219

Munro, E. (2019). Decision-making under uncertainty in child protection: Creating a just and learning culture. *Child & Family Social Work*, *24*(1), 123–130. https://doi.org/10.1111/cfs.12589

Murphy, P. R., & Poist, R. F. (1992). The Logistics-Marketing Interference: Techniques for Enhancing Cooperation. *Transportation Journal (American Society of Transportation & Logistics Inc)*, *32*(2), 14–23.

Neuman, M. (1991). Utopia, dystopia, diaspora. *Journal of the American Planning Association*, *57*(3), 344. https://doi.org/10.1080/01944369108975505

Nietzsche, F. (1968). *The will to power.* Vintage Books.

Nilsen, C., Andel, R., Fors, S., Meinow, B., Mattsson, A. D., & Kåreholt, I. (2014). Associations between work-related stress in late midlife, educational attainment, and serious health problems in old age: a longitudinal study with over 20 years of follow-up. *BMC Public Health*, *14*, 1–12. https://doi.org/10.1186/1471-2458-14-878

Nuesiri, E. O. (2016). Decentralised forest management: towards a utopian realism. *Geographical Journal*, *182*(1), 97–103. https://doi.org/10.1111/geoj.12104

Odermatt, I., König, C. J., Kleinmann, M., Bachmann, M., Röder, H., & Schmitz, P. (2018). Incivility in Meetings: Predictors and Outcomes. *Journal of Business & Psychology*, *33*(2), 263–282. https://doi.org/10.1007/s10869-017-9490-0

Parker, M. (1998). Organisation, Community and Utopia. *Studies in Cultures, Organizations & Societies*, *4*(1), 71. https://doi.org/10.1080/10245289808523504

Parker, M. (2015). Between sociology and the business school: critical studies of work, employment and organization in the UK. *Sociological Review*, *63*(1), 162–180. https://doi.org/10.1111/1467-954X.12166

Paul, R. J., Niehoff, B. P., & Turnley, W. H. (2000). Empowerment, expectations, and the psychological contract--managing the dilemmas and gaining the advantages. *Journal of Socio-Economics*, *29*(5), 471. https://doi.org/10.1016/S1053-5357(00)00083-4

Paulsson, A. (2011). Resisting self-management? On the possibility of dissolving oneself in fast food restaurants. *Ephemera: Theory & Politics in Organization*, *11*(2), 122–137.

Pelletier-Bosshard, E., Freeman, A., Jauvin, N., & Côté, N. (2021). Strategies Used by Middle Managers to Support Employees Carrying Out Emotionally Demanding Work: Which Strategies and Why Those Ones? *RELATIONS INDUSTRIELLES-INDUSTRIAL RELATIONS*, *76*(1), 143–165.

Pfeffer, J. (1992). Understanding Power in Organizations. *California Management Review*, *34*(2), 29–50. https://doi.org/10.2307/41166692

Pfrombeck, J., Doden, W., Grote, G., & Feierabend, A. (2020). A study of organizational cynicism and how it is affected by social exchange relationships at work. *Journal of Occupational & Organizational Psychology*, *93*(3), 578–604. https://doi.org/10.1111/joop.12306

Prasad, A., & Prasad, P. (1993). Reconceptualizing Alienation in Management Inquiry. *Journal of Management Inquiry*, *2*(2), 169–183. https://doi.org/10.1177/105649269322007

Pretorius, S., Steyn, H., & Bond-Barnard, T. J. (2018). Leadership Styles in Projects: Current Trends and Future Opportunities. *South African Journal of Industrial Engineering, 29*(3), 161–172. https://doi.org/10.7166/29-3-2057

Pugh, S. D., Skarlicki, D. P., & Passell, B. S. (2003). After the fall: Layoff victims' trust and cynicism in re-employment. *Journal of Occupational & Organizational Psychology, 76*(2), 201. https://doi.org/10.1348/096317903765913704

Quinn, B. (2007). Turning out the Light. *Pollution Engineering, 39*(7), 16.

Rahim, E. (2011). Implications of Open-source Social Networking on Entrepreneurship. *International Journal of Technology, Knowledge & Society, 7*(4), 45–56.

Ramírez, R. R., Alarcón, L. F. C., & Knights, P. (2004). Benchmarking System for Evaluating Management Practices in the Construction Industry. *Journal of Management in Engineering, 20*(3), 110–117. https://doi.org/10.1061/(ASCE)0742-597X(2004)20:3(110)

Ranasinghe, P., Wathurapatha, W. S., Perera, Y. S., Lamabadusuriya, D. A., Kulatunga, S., Jayawardana, N., & Katulanda, P. (2016). Computer vision syndrome among computer office workers in a developing country: an evaluation of prevalence and risk factors. *BMC Research Notes, 9*, 1–9. https://doi.org/10.1186/s13104-016-1962-1

Reineholm, C., Gustavsson, M., Liljegren, M., & Ekberg, K. (2012). The importance of work conditions and health for voluntary job mobility: a two-year follow-up. *BMC Public Health, 12*(1), 682–688. https://doi.org/10.1186/1471-2458-12-682

Robson, S. M., & Hansson, R. O. (2007). Strategic Self Development for Successful Aging at Work. *International Journal of Aging & Human Development*, *64*(4), 331–359. https://doi.org/10.2190/Q303-171U-7686-8517

Sartre, J.-P. (2007). *Existentialism is a humanism*. Yale University Pres.

Sawhney, G., & Michel, J. S. (2021). Challenge and Hindrance Stressors and Work Outcomes: The Moderating Role of Day-Level Affect. *Journal of Business & Psychology*, 1–17. https://doi.org/10.1007/s10869-021-09752-5

Scalliet, P. (2006). Risk, society and system failure. *Radiotherapy & Oncology*, *80*(3), 275–281. https://doi.org/10.1016/j.radonc.2006.07.003

Schilling, E. (2015). "Success Is Satisfaction with What You Have"? Biographical Work-Life Balance of Older Female Employees in Public Administration. *Gender, Work & Organization*, *22*(5), 474–494. https://doi.org/10.1111/gwao.12097

Schmitz, L. L., McCluney, C. L., Sonnega, A., & Hicken, M. T. (2019). Policy Levers May Improve Older Workers' Perceptions of Their Psychosocial Work Environment: Research findings show that workplace policies can play a crucial role in the quality of older worker's health and job longevity. *Generations*, *43*(3), 78–85.

Shantz, A., Alfes, K., & Truss, C. (2014). Alienation from work: Marxist ideologies and twenty-first-century practice. *International Journal of Human Resource Management*, *25*(18), 2529–2550. https://doi.org/10.1080/09585192.2012.667431

Sharma, S. K., Kaur, J., Kaur, R., & Kaur, R. (2014). Employment Pattern and Health Profile of Elderly. *Baba Farid University Nursing Journal*, *6*(1), 85–88.

Shoubo Xu, & Li Da Xu. (2011). Management: a scientific discipline for humanity. *Information Technology & Management, 12*(2), 51–54. https://doi.org/10.1007/s10799-011-0090-9

Sihag, A. (2016). Factors affecting employee motivation for organizational effectiveness health care employees. *Indian Journal of Positive Psychology, 7*(2), 256–260.

Skok, M. M., Zoroja, J., & Bach, M. P. (2013). Simulation Modelling Approach to Human Resources Management: Burnout Effect Case Study. *Interdisciplinary Description of Complex Systems, 11*(3), 277–288. https://doi.org/10.7906/indecs.11.3.4

Sloterdijk, P. (1987). *Critique of cynical reason.* University of Minnesota Press.

Sułkowski, Ł. (2011). About utopias in management. *Contemporary Management Quarterly / Wspólczesne Zarzadzanie, 4*, 23–33.

Terpstra, D. E., & Rozell, E. J. (1998). Human Resource Executives' Perceptions of Academic Research. *Journal of Business & Psychology, 13*(1), 19–29. https://doi.org/10.1023/A:1022914931475

Torres, C. (2005). Dividends & interest: At a leader's peril: Lies, lies, and half-truths. *Leadership in Action, 25*(4), 25–26.

Um-e-Rubbab, & Naqvi, S. M. M. R. (2020). Employee voice behavior as a critical factor for organizational sustainability in the telecommunications industry. *PLoS ONE, 15*(9), 1–17. https://doi.org/10.1371/journal.pone.0238451

Vanderstukken, A., & Caniels, M. C. J. (2021). Predictors of work alienation: differences between hierarchical levels. *Career Development International, 26*(5), 640-656. https://doi.org/10.1108/CDI-01-2021-0013

Welch, A. V., Williams, P. S., Darville, R., Smartt, P., & McBroom, M. (2015). Exploratory Research on Changing Times

Affecting Human Resource Management, Perceptions, and Professional Norms of Tennessee Park Rangers. *Journal of Park & Recreation Administration, 33*(1), 72–92.

Wesner, B., Smith, A., & Austin, T. (2018). Ready for action: Developing classroom teams to prepare students for the business world. *Administrative Issues Journal: Education, Practice & Research, 8*(2), 119–137. https://doi.org/10.5929/2019.1.14.9

Westgate, C., Musoke, D., Crigler, L., & Perry, H. B. (2021). Community health workers at the dawn of a new era: 7. Recent advances in supervision. *Health Research Policy & Systems, 19*, 1–18. https://doi.org/10.1186/s12961-021-00754-6

Wiggins, C. B. (2008). "He's Such a Jerk!!" Education as a Response to Professionally Inappropriate Behavior. *Hamline Journal of Public Law & Policy, 29*(2), 299–315.

Willmott, H. (2013). Reflections on the Darker Side of Conventional Power Analytics. *Academy of Management Perspectives, 27*(4), 281–286. https://doi.org/10.5465/amp.2013.0075

Xiang, L., Low, A. H. L., Leung, Y. Y., Fong, W., Gan, W. H., Graves, N., & Thumboo, J. (2020). Work disability in rheumatic diseases: Baseline results from an inception cohort. *International Journal of Rheumatic Diseases, 23*(8), 1040–1049. https://doi.org/10.1111/1756-185X.13864

Yoon, J., Kim, M., & Shin, J. (2016). Confidence in delegation and leadership of registered nurses in long-term-care hospitals. *Journal of Nursing Management (John Wiley & Sons, Inc.), 24*(5), 676–685. https://doi.org/10.1111/jonm.12372

Žižek, S. (2009). *The sublime object of ideology: The essential Žižek.* Verso.

Author Biography

Ross Jackson has over twenty years of experience in applied analytics and strategy development in both bureaucratic organizations and small startups. He has taught strategy and management in large for-profit universities and small liberal arts colleges. An author of over thirty publications, his works include *Haunted Across the Political Spectrum: The Specter of Communism in Two Midcentury American Organizations*, *Nietzsche's Construction of Power: Implications for International Business Ethics*, *Becoming Who You Are Through Authentic Organizational Communication*, and *The Spectacle of Analysis: Analytics as Organizational Propaganda*. His research interests include the linguistic and existential facets of organizing, power, and the potential intersectionality among analysis, data visualization, and détournement.

Made in the USA
Monee, IL
06 December 2022

20013651R10089